TOTAL YOUTH MINISTRY

MINISTRY RESOURCES FOR

Justice and Service

Pray It! Study It! Live It!™ resources offer a holistic approach
to learning, living, and passing on the Catholic faith.

The Total Faith™ Initiative

Total Catechesis
Catechetical Sessions on Christian Morality
Catechetical Sessions on Christian Prayer
Catechetical Sessions on Liturgy and the Sacraments
Catechetical Sessions on the Creed

Total Youth Ministry
Ministry Resources for Community Life
Ministry Resources for Evangelization
Ministry Resources for Justice and Service
Ministry Resources for Pastoral Care
Ministry Resources for Prayer and Worship
Ministry Resources for Youth Leadership Development

Total Faith™ Initiative Coordinator's Manual

The Catholic Faith Handbook for Youth

The Catholic Youth Bible™

TOTAL YOUTH MINISTRY

MINISTRY RESOURCES FOR

Justice and Service

Thomas J. Bright, Sean T. Lansing,
Mike Poulin and Joan Weber

saint mary's press

To the poor, marginalized, and voiceless, who are the motivation for this resource and who inspire us by their faith and courage in the face of adversity.

The publishing team included Barbara Murray and Laurie Delgatto, development editors; Barbara Bartelson, production editor; Cären Yang, art director and designer; Jonathan Thomas Goebel, cover designer; Digital Images © PhotoDisc, Inc., cover images; Alan S. Hanson, prepress specialist; Elly Poppe, CD-ROM developer; manufacturing coordinated by the production services department of Saint Mary's Press.

The contributors to this resource manual include Valeria Spinner-Banks and Marian Lamoureux, who assisted with the extended session on *Racism: Our Response.*

Produced with the assistance of settingPace, LLC.

Ministry Resource manuals were developed in collaboration with the Center for Ministry Development. The publishing team included Joan Weber, manual editor; Thomas East, project coordinator; and Cheryl Tholcke, content editor.

Printed in the United States of America

2462

ISBN 978-0-88489-773-6

Contents

Introduction

About Total Youth Ministry

Many youth today are waiting to hear the Good News that is ours as Christ's disciples. Youth in our parishes long to grow spiritually and to belong to their family, Church, and local community in meaningful ways. Parents of youth long to experience Church as supportive of and caring about the same things they care about. They hope the parish will offer ways for youth to be involved and to grow in their faith. Parents want to understand youth ministry so they can support and encourage their child's participation.

Parishes want to know how to include youth and how to pass on faith to a new generation. Parish members want to see youth more involved, and are worried about the challenges that face today's youth. They know that young people need support from their faith community—now more than ever. Parish youth ministry leaders are generous, passionate, and busy people; they make sacrifices so that youth will have a community to belong to and a place to grow. They need ideas and plans for youth ministry activities—and strategies that really work. They are working toward a ministry that goes beyond just gathering groups of young people; they are working toward a ministry that makes connections between youth and the community.

All those voices have something in common—a longing for youth ministry that is inclusive, dynamic, and flexible.

In 1997 the United States Conference of Catholic Bishops (USCCB) published its blueprint for youth ministry in the twenty-first century. *Renewing the Vision: A Framework for Catholic Youth Ministry* challenges youth ministry to focus its efforts in these directions:

- to empower young people to live as disciples of Jesus Christ in our world today
- to draw young people to responsible participation in the life, mission, and work of the Catholic faith community
- to foster the total personal and spiritual growth of each young person

In *Renewing the Vision*, the bishops urge the Church to guide young people toward a life of fullness in Jesus Christ, and to give them the tools that will enable them to live out that fullness as Catholic Christians. To put it simply, the bishops call young people to embrace their faith as they study it, pray it, and live it. The bishops also challenge the faith community to surround young people with love, care, and attention and to include youth throughout the life of the parish.

The Ministry Resource Manuals

The ministry resource manuals of the Total Youth Ministry series address each of the components of youth ministry as outlined in *Renewing the Vision*. The advocacy and catechesis components are woven throughout the ministry resource manuals. You will find the following information in each of the ministry resource manuals:

- a chapter explaining the component, connecting it to Church documents, and identifying practical ideas and resources for implementing the component
- sessions that can stand alone or be combined with others in the series
- numerous strategies, ideas, suggestions, and resources that go beyond a specific gathering

The content of each manual includes newly developed sessions, ideas and strategies as well as "tried and true" material drawn or adapted from *YouthWorks* and other resources previously published by the Center for Ministry Development.

Following is a brief description of each of the manuals:

- *Ministry Resources for Community Life* offers faith communities program resources and strategies to build community among young people and throughout the entire parish. The resource includes nine gathered sessions to help young people get to know one another, themselves, and the meaning of Christian community. It also contains an outline for an ecumenical event to help build community across denominational lines, and it offers practical strategies and ideas to help manage community issues, make the most of community life opportunities, and encourage intergenerational and family relationships.
- *Ministry Resources for Evangelization* offers faith communities tools and program resources to evangelize youth. It offers practical strategies and ideas for outreach to young people and contains twelve gathered sessions to share the Good News. It also includes a retreat to engage young people in becoming or continuing as Jesus' disciples.
- *Ministry Resources for Justice and Service* offers faith communities programs and strategies to engage youth in justice, direct service, and advocacy in faithful, age-appropriate, and proactive ways. This resource contains eight gathered sessions around specific justice issues, an overnight retreat on service to poor people, and two half-day retreats or evening reflections on simplicity and racism.

- At the heart of *Ministry Resources for Pastoral Care* are twelve sessions designed to equip young people with the tools needed to celebrate their holy goodness and navigate some of life's difficult issues. The topics of the sessions include recognizing the goodness in oneself and others, building and maintaining relationships, dealing with tough times, and preparing for the future. The last section of the manual comprises strategies for doing the ongoing work of pastoral care.
- *Ministry Resources for Prayer and Worship* is designed for those who work with and walk with youth in this journey of discipleship. The manual contains three sessions to teach youth to pray and to practice praying in different forms. Eleven communal prayer services are included, which can be used on a variety of occasions throughout the seasons of the year. The manual also contains strategies and resources to help youth communities develop patterns of prayer and to include youth in preparing prayers and liturgies.
- *Ministry Resources for Youth Leadership Development* offers faith communities program resources and strategies to develop youth as leaders within youth ministry programs and the parish. The manual includes four foundational sessions on Christian leadership, ten leadership skill sessions and minisessions, and two sessions to help prepare youth and adults for working together. The manual offers ideas and strategies for creating leadership roles within the parish, inviting youth to leadership, and working with the parents of youth leaders. The plans for implementing sessions and other gathered events are complete, easy to follow, and adaptable to your community.

With the detailed plans provided for the sessions, activities, and strategies in Total Youth Ministry, youth ministry volunteers no longer need to be program designers. By using the Total Youth Ministry resources, you can focus on the important task of finding the leaders who make youth ministry happen. Each session includes an overview, a list of materials, preparation steps, and step-by-step instructions for facilitating a session with confidence. Most sessions also include a variety of ways to extend the theme of the session with prayer, related learning exercises, or follow-through experiences.

An Added Feature: CD-ROMs

Each manual has a CD-ROM that includes the full content of the manual and is in read-only, non-print format. Handouts are provided in printable color versions (which cannot be customized) and in black-and-white versions that you can customize for the particular needs of a group. You will also find hyperlinks to suggested Web sites.

Participant Resources

Much of the material in the ministry resource manuals is designed to work in a complementary way with the contents of *The Catholic Faith Handbook for Youth (CFH)* and *The Catholic Youth Bible (CYB)*.

Ministry Resources for Justice and Service: An Overview

Ministry Resources for Justice and Service offers faith communities program resources and strategies to engage youth in justice, direct service, and advocacy. This resource contains eight gathered sessions around specific justice issues, an overnight retreat on service to the poor, and two half-day retreats or evening reflections on simplicity and racism. All the sessions utilize the pastoral circle process to immerse youth in a justice issue, educate them on the "why" of injustice, help them reflect on the issue from a faith perspective, and support them in choosing a faith response to combat injustice. The resource also offers practical strategies for engaging youth in the work of justice, service, and advocacy in faithful, age-appropriate and pro-active ways.

Manual Contents: An Overview

Part A: Living Discipleship Today Through Service, Justice, and Advocacy for People in Need

Part A of the manual explores the central concepts of service, justice, and advocacy. It explains the process of involving young people in direct service through preparation, engagement, reflection, and celebration. It also includes an explanation of the pastoral circle process, which engages people in seeking justice through involvement, social analysis, theological reflection, and action. This part also lists suggested resources for the adult facilitator on Catholic social teaching and current justice issues.

Part B: Pastoral Circle Justice Sessions

The justice sessions include opportunities for young people to learn more about justice issues and to explore the Scriptures and Catholic social teachings' call to serve the poor and to stand up to injustice. You may choose to use the material in this section in its entirety, or you may select sessions that you think will be best for the young people with whom you work. The sessions are not sequential, so you may organize them in the way that is most appropriate for your situation.

Each session begins with a brief overview, a list of expected outcomes, the core session at a glance, the necessary materials, and the preparation required by the facilitator. Within the session is a complete description of its procedures, including the four movements of involvement, exploration, reflection, and action possibilities. Closing prayer follows.

Related Scriptural passages, *CYB* articles, and musical selections from *Spirit & Song* are provided when appropriate. Some of the sessions provide a list of media resources—such as print, movie, and Internet—for more exploration. Family approaches provide simple follow-up suggestions for family learning, prayer, and service. In addition, all the activities can be enhanced by the creativity and expertise of the adult leader.

Session Overviews

Chapter 2: A Catholic Approach to Justice and Service

- This session helps participants explore the wisdom found in the Church's social teaching and examine how it can be used to guide their involvement with people in need today.

Chapter 3: Life: Who Gets to Choose?

- This session engages the participants in examining their opinions and feelings about a particular life issue—the death penalty—then puts them in dialogue with the Church's seamless garment approach to all life issues.

Chapter 4: Children's Rights: National, Global and Galactic

- This session helps participants explore the meaning of children's rights and apply what they learn from international conventions and the wisdom of the Church to the situation of children in need.

Chapter 5: Exactly What Is a Just Wage?

- In this session, participants see the connection between their own work experience as an employee and that of the working poor, examine wages, learn how much a dollar buys, and learn how much money a family must earn to live above the poverty line. Participants also look at what the Church teaches about just wages and work.

Chapter 6: Working for the Common Good

- This session explores the theme of the common good as a basic tenet of Catholic social teaching and makes participants aware of the power they have to bring about positive change in the world.

Chapter 7: Caring for Creation: Environmental Justice

- In this session participants examine the environment that surrounds them; explore the dangers that threaten the environment locally, nationally, and internationally; and reflect on an environmental statement from the U.S. Catholic Bishops.

Chapter 8: How Can War Be Justified?

- This session explores what it means to follow the God of peace and do God's will in an imperfect world. Participants explore the concepts of nonviolence and just war as faith responses to the disregard for human dignity and human rights.

Chapter 9: Hunger Among Us

- This session helps participants explore the reality of hunger, take an initial step in being part of the solution, and learn options for where their concerns can lead them.

Part C: Justice Retreats and Extended Sessions Using the Pastoral Circle Process

Retreats Overview

Chapter 10: Responding in Service to the Needs of the Poor (An Overnight Retreat Experience)

- This retreat experience helps participants understand the causes and consequences of poverty for individuals and society, and respond in faithful service to the needs of the poor. The retreat format allows concentrated time to learn, reflect, and serve.

Chapter 11: Simplicity or Stuff: Which Will You Choose? A Lenten Evening Reflection

- This session is designed as a Lenten evening reflection to engage youth in examining their lives in light of the Gospel challenges to pray, fast, and give alms. Using a justice perspective, the facilitator leads the young people through activities, which place their own spending and consumption habits in relationship to what others have and lack.

Chapter 12: Racism: Our Response (A Half-Day Retreat)

- This session investigates the ways the participants can respond to racism as Catholic Christians. The session begins with a simulation game designed to illustrate the many issues that surface when we interact with cultures that are unfamiliar. Large-group and small-group discussions help the participants reflect on their own experiences with racism and begin to name some action steps they can take to combat racism.

Part D: Strategies for Justice and Service Work with Youth

Engaging young people in the social ministry of the Church is not optional—it is demanded by the Gospel and our Catholic faith. This section of the manual includes strategies, both gathered and non-gathered, for connecting young people with justice and service through a faith perspective. The strategies' design supports you in providing service experiences, service learning, advocacy, and cultural awareness to youth. The strategies are not sequential or programmatic. They suggest ideas to strengthen the justice work you are currently doing or are the catalyst for stretching into new areas of justice you have never before explored with the young people of your parish.

Chapter 13: Planning Effective Service Projects with Youth
- This strategy offers helpful insights for planning and implementing service projects with young people. In addition it gives concrete suggestions for evaluating and choosing appropriate service agencies and work sites.

Chapter 14: Researching a Justice Issue
- Practical methods and actual sources for conducting preliminary research on justice and service topics are the basis of this strategy. The strategy covers ideas for engaging youth in the research personally, as well.

Chapter 15: Doing Advocacy with Youth
- Suggestions, tools, and resources for adding advocacy to all direct service programs or conducting advocacy strategies independent of service projects make up this strategy.

Chapter 16: Using Scripture to Educate Youth in Justice and Service
- Suggestions for resources and methods that engage young people in exploring the scriptural foundations of justice issues are found in this strategy.

Chapter 17: Preparing Speakers and Panel Members to Educate Youth in Justice
- Included in this strategy are practical tips for selecting and preparing speakers who will inspire and motivate young people to take action against injustice.

Chapter 18: Learning from Other Cultures
- This strategy offers ideas to inform young people of the richness of diversity by engaging them in family traditions, the local community's traditions, and ethnic calendar events and celebrations.

Chapter 19: Using Calendar Connections through the Year
- This strategy offers ways to connect liturgical and secular calendar events to create in young people a deeper awareness of their Catholic identity and of justice issues.

Chapter 20: Recognizing and Celebrating Youth Service
- Provided in this strategy are ways to honor the service of young people and to celebrate their discipleship in action.

Handouts and Resources

All the necessary handouts and resources are found at the end of each chapter in the manual. They are also found on the accompanying CD-ROM, in both color and black-and-white versions. The black-and-white materials may be customized to suit your particular needs.

Facilitating the Sessions

Preparing Yourself

Read each session or activity before you facilitate it. Pay attention to what is happening in your community, in our nation, or in the world regarding the justice topic being studied. You will want to become acquainted with the various Catholic social documents that address the issue. Then use the information creatively to meet the needs of the young people in your group. Knowing your audience will help you determine which strategies will work best for it. Some of the activities require preparation. Allow yourself adequate time to get ready.

Presentations

In each session, leaders will be asked to make short presentations to the young people. Ensure that these presentations are effective by practicing them ahead of time, personalizing the materials by adding your own stories and examples, familiarizing yourself with the material, and inviting constructive criticism from other leaders.

Social Teaching Library

Getting youth in direct contact with the social teachings of our Church can be a source of inspiration, pride, and deepened Catholic identity. Consider developing a library of social documents (encyclicals and pastoral letters), as well as *Catholic Updates* and *Youth Updates,* which summarize the contemporary social teachings of our pope and bishops.

Standard Materials

To save time, consider gathering frequently used materials in bins and storing those bins in a place that is accessible to all staff and volunteer leaders. Here are some recommendations for organizing the bins.

Supply Bin

The following items appear frequently in the materials checklists:
- *The Catholic Youth Bible,* at least one copy for each participant
- *The Catholic Faith Handbook for Youth,* for your reference as leader
- masking tape
- cellophane tape
- washable and permanent markers (thick-line and thin-line)
- pens or pencils
- self-stick notes
- scissors
- newsprint
- blank paper, scrap paper, and notebook paper

- journals, one for each participant
- index cards
- baskets
- candles and matches
- items to create a prayer space (for example, a colored cloth, a cross, a bowl of water, and a vase for flowers)

Music Bin

Young people often find profound meaning in the music and lyrics of songs, both past and present. Also, the right music can set the appropriate mood for a prayer or an activity. Begin with a small collection of tapes or CDs in a music bin, and add to it over time. You might ask the young people to put some of their favorite music in the bin. The bin might include the following styles of music:

- *Prayerful, reflective instrumental music,* such as the kind that is available in the adult alternative section of music stores. Labels that specialize in this type of music include Windham Hill and Narada.
- *Popular songs with powerful messages.* If you are not well versed in popular music, ask the young people to offer suggestions.
- *The music of contemporary Catholic artists.* Many teens are familiar with the work of Catholic musicians such as Steve Angrisano, Sarah Hart, David W. Kauffman, Michael Mahler, Jesse Manibusan, and Danielle Rose.

Also consider including songbooks and hymnals. Many of the musical selections suggested in Total Youth Ministry are taken from the *Spirit & Song* hymnal, published by Oregon Catholic Press (OCP). If you wish to order copies of this hymnal, please contact OCP directly at *www.ocp.org* or by calling 800-548-8749. Including copies of your parish's chosen hymnal is a suitable option as well. You might also check with your liturgy or music director for recordings of parish hymns.

Some Closing Thoughts

We hope you find this material helpful as you invite young people into a deeper relationship with the marvelous community of faith we know as the Catholic Church. Please be assured of our continual prayers for you and the young people you serve.

Your Comments or Suggestions

Saint Mary's Press wants to know your reactions to the materials in the Total Youth Ministry series. We are open to all kinds of suggestions, including these:

- an alternative way to conduct an activity
- an audiovisual or other media resource that worked well with this material
- a book or an article you found helpful
- an original activity or process
- a prayer experience or service
- a helpful preparation for other leaders
- an observation about the themes or content of this material

If you have a comment or suggestion, please write to us at 702 Terrace Heights, Winona, MN 55987-1318; call us at our toll-free number, 800-533-8095; or e-mail us at *smp@smp.org*. Your ideas will help improve future editions of Total Youth Ministry.

Living as Disciples Today Through Service, Justice, and Advocacy

Justice:
A Catholic Priority

Our faith calls us to work for justice; to serve those in need; to pursue peace; and to defend the life, dignity, and rights of all our sisters and brothers. This is the call of Jesus, the challenge of the prophets, and the living tradition of our Church.

> (United States Conference of Catholic Bishops,
> *A Century of Social Teaching*, p. 1)

With these powerful words, the United States Conference of Catholic Bishops (USCCB) challenges the Church in the United States of America to reflect on its long tradition of service and to strengthen its commitment to work for real peace and justice in our world. The bishops remind us that serving the needy and speaking for the voiceless are not new and peripheral but ancient and central to our faith.

The Church's social ministry is, in their words:

Founded on the life and words of Jesus Christ . . . inspired by the passion for justice of the Hebrew prophets . . . shaped by the social teaching of our Church . . . and . . . lived by the People of God, who seek to build up the kingdom of God, to live our faith in the world, and to apply the values of the Scriptures and the teaching of the Church in our own families and parishes, in our work and service, and in local communities, the nation, and the world.

> (*A Century of Social Teaching*, pp. 2–3)

This call to justice and service is echoed throughout local, national, and international Church documents. It is little wonder that justice and service receives so much energy and attention in *Renewing the Vision: A Framework for Catholic Youth Ministry,* the bishops' statement on ministry with youth (Washington, DC: USCCB, 1997).

Renewing the Vision invites young people to participate in an adventure that is spiritually challenging and world changing—living as disciples of

What Do You Think?

How much of a priority are justice and service in your faith community?

Jesus in our world. Empowering young people for this task is, accordingly, the first of three interlocking goals for the Church's ministry with youth.

> Ministry with adolescents helps young people learn what it means to follow Jesus Christ and to live as his disciples today, empowering them to serve others and to work toward a world built on the vision and values of the reign of God (p. 9).

The call to discipleship through justice and service is explored in depth in *Renewing the Vision* in the ministry components of Justice and Service and of Advocacy. A summary of the document's teaching in these areas follows this Introduction. To help the facilitator prepare young people for discipleship, give him or her resource 1, "A Summary of Key Points from *Renewing the Vision*." Justice, service, and advocacy play an important role in ministry with young people precisely because they are essential parts of the Church's overall ministry. Our efforts with young people need to do more than expose them to the problems experienced by the people around them. We must also empower young people to change the situations that harm and oppress others. Discipleship demands no less than this. Direct service, action on behalf of justice, and advocacy for those in need offer different avenues for making this change a reality. Together they serve as powerful tools for making God's Kingdom more of a reality in our time.

Direct Service

It was Anna's first time at the soup kitchen. She was there as part of a Confirmation service project, but she had wanted to go for a long time. Her group had put lots of time into preparation, but, even so the experience was different than she had expected. There seemed to be hundreds to feed . . . and so many of them were kids! Anna was shy at first, but it didn't take long for her usual smile and sense of humor to surface, and then she started to enjoy herself. Everyone got a piece of pie and an accompanying smile—and her smile proved contagious. When the line at the counter dwindled, Anna and her friend Kristin went into the dining room and started playing with the young kids. Their mothers enjoyed the break and started talking among themselves but eventually drew Anna and Kristin into the conversation. Too soon, it was time for Anna and her friends to leave. As she left, Anna realized that this was one of the best Saturday mornings in quite a while. She helped folks at the kitchen, had a great time, and was going home conscious of how much she had to be thankful for. Wouldn't her family be surprised! She was ready to come again as soon as she could. If the Confirmation group wasn't returning, maybe she and Kristin could get their parents to go. Or maybe they would just try it on their own.

What Do You Think?

◆ Who mentored you into discipleship?

◆ What experiences compelled you to serve others and change the world?

What Do You Think?

What direct service opportunities are available in your parish?

Direct service exposes young people to the realities of suffering and need and helps in alleviating the problems. Matthew's account of the last judgment (25:31–46) leaves little doubt that Jesus identifies with the poor in their suffering and want and expects an immediate response to their need. Direct service takes a variety of forms. In the case of hunger or malnutrition, for example, actions of direct service could include any or all of the following:

- organizing a food drive to restock the shelves of the local food pantry
- preparing a homemade meal for residents of a homeless shelter
- sending in regular financial contributions to keep the shelter or soup kitchen in operation
- making parishioners aware of the needs of local, national, or international agencies dedicated to hunger relief

Direct service benefits everyone involved. It gives young people the opportunity to put a human face to the needs they have heard about, do something that makes a difference for the good, appreciate how their talents and resources can be used to serve others, and draw the connection between discipleship and the needs of the poor. Direct service also benefits the groups and agencies served. Most relief agencies rely heavily on volunteers to make their work possible. Young people not only fill a particular time slot or need but also bring a sense of renewed hope and joy to staff members and volunteers, who live with the consequences of need on a daily basis.

These benefits do not come automatically with direct service but necessitate conscious planning and preparation. In its most effective form, direct service involves four distinct phases: Prepare, Engage, Reflect, and Celebrate.

Prepare

Young people should be aware of the needs they are to respond to and how these needs affect the lives of poor people. They need to know what they are likely to experience, what is expected of them, and how to do it. Good preparation provides young people with the knowledge and skills to empower them for success. For example, if you take young people to a nursing home to visit the residents, it would be beneficial to bring in the social director of the home to prepare the youth for the experience. The director could address the home's sights, smells, and settings, talk about what life is like for the residents, share ideas for the focus of conversations, and encourage them to visit in pairs rather than alone. If the director emphasizes that their presence itself is a gift to the residents, young people will enter the experience much more relaxed and empowered to share their youthful energy with the residents.

Engage

Having a caring adult or experienced young person accompany the youth encourages them to enter into the experience fully. The role of ministry leaders on-site is to equip, empower, and support youth, not to do their work. The role of the leader may vary from experience to experience. Sometimes leaders need to be role models for the young people, especially when the youth are doing a service they have never done before. For example, if young people are working with AIDS patients, seeing the leader take one patient's hands and engage in conversation with that patient could mitigate the young people's hesitations or fears. At other times, the leader should step back and let the young people fully immerse themselves in the service experience. An example of this might be serving in a soup kitchen and talking to guests at the end of the meal. Rather than taking over and doing all the talking, the leader might be wise to let the youth feel their way through the experience.

What Do You Think?

How do you make the connections with youth between the service they do and the faith they profess?

Reflect

When young people go through a service project that confronts them with issues they have never personally experienced, they need to reflect on what has happened around and within them during the engagement phase. Reflection helps young people own what they have learned through service about the issues, about the people involved, about themselves, and about discipleship. Reflection can take the form of a few simple journal questions, a quiet conversation with the leader and the other participants in the car or van on the way home, or an activity back at the parish or school designed to put them in touch with their feelings, thoughts, and choices for future involvement.

Celebrate

Recognizing and celebrating service helps young people know they are a gifted and valued part of the community. It can also serve as a catalyst for families and parishioners to reflect on their commitments to service and to rededicate themselves to discipleship through serving the needs of the poor.

Justice

Robert and his family have been volunteering at the homeless shelter for about a year. They help staff the shelter kitchen one night a month. The first few times they came, they were too busy getting food on the counter to pay attention to everything that was happening around them. By now, though, things are different. They are comfortable with the kitchen routine and know some of the "regulars" by name and attitude—

who likes to talk and who doesn't, who has a joke or smile to share, and who always asks for double dessert! Some of the regulars at the shelter aren't much older than Robert, a fact that he finds hard to understand. Like almost everyone else, they are polite and dress okay. If he had run into them at the mall, he never would have known they were shelter guests. He figures he shouldn't ask, but he would like to know their stories. How did they end up at the shelter? Why were they still here? What did they need to make it on their own? Robert likes to have people he knows around, but somehow he hopes these guests will be gone soon—for their own sake. Otherwise it would get pretty depressing here.

Responding through direct service to people's immediate need for assistance or support, valuable as it is, is not sufficient to banish the problems for good. It does little to change the situations that created the need in the first place. As disciples of Jesus, we must be about justice *and* service, alleviating people's current suffering *and* working to limit and eliminate the causes of the suffering.

As happened above in Robert's case, direct service often becomes an entrée to justice for young people. Justice takes us a step deeper, asking us to discover and dismantle the beliefs and behaviors, structures and systems that allow poverty and need to endure. Like direct service, justice can take a variety of forms. In the case of hunger, the issue referenced above, justice could involve young people in any of the following ways:

- working with groups and agencies that give individuals more control over their own lives (Habitat for Humanity, Heifer Project International)
- supporting Neighborhood Watch and violence prevention programs
- babysitting for parents engaged in education or citizenship classes
- raising funds for development agencies (Catholic Campaign for Human Development, Catholic Relief Services)
- making families and parishioners aware of both the causes of need and the agencies committed to promoting change

Education Sessions

Catechetical and service programs alike help young people look beyond the immediate need to the reasons behind it. The education sessions offered in this resource manual provide a solid approach to helping young people move from awareness to action on justice issues. The approach used in the sessions is called the Pastoral Circle and consists of four movements:

Involvement

This movement helps the young people get an "insider perspective" on the issue by examining their current beliefs and experiences and comparing them with the real-life experience of those entangled in the issue today.

What Do You Think?

What has your faith community done to move your young people from direct service to action on behalf of justice?

Exploration

This movement invites the young people to look beyond the immediate need of an issue and focus on its causes, by examining the *reality* of the issue (numbers and population affected), the *reasons* it exists (history, power and control, values, assumptions, and prejudices), and the *resources* necessary to respond adequately to the need.

Reflection

In this movement the young people compare and contrast a current situation with the vision offered by faith. The movement includes assessing what the Scriptures and Church teaching, the witness of believers, and the organized activity of the Church have to say about the issue.

Action

In this final movement, the young people begin to make a difference, moving out in direct service and justice, speaking on behalf of those in need, working as individuals, families, and a community to help today's reality conform more closely to the Kingdom of God proclaimed by Jesus.

Advocacy

Anna and Robert shared lots in common, including an ongoing commitment to service. To them, the "poor" weren't statistics but people they knew personally and considered friends. Anna and Robert had recently celebrated their 18th birthdays and were looking forward to the chance to vote. Their service work had convinced them that handing out food, as necessary as it was, was not enough to solve hunger and homelessness. They wanted to change the things that hurt the people they had come to know, and they figured that politics was a good place to start. So they checked out what the different candidates for mayor and city council had to say about the issues and talked together about how their votes could make a difference in the life of poor people. They decided to share their concerns with their other friends to attempt to multiply the number of people who vote with the needs of the poor in mind.

Speaking out on social issues and promoting effective change move us into a third form of action, namely, advocacy. In *Renewing the Vision,* advocacy carries a dual focus:

- calling on the Church to examine "how well young people are integrated into [its] life, mission, and work" (p. 27)
- challenging the community to marshal its "resources and talents . . . to shape a society [that is] more respectful of the life, dignity, and rights of [young people] and their families" (p. 27)

Advocacy can range from speaking and voting according to your values to using purchasing decisions and power to make your beliefs known. It involves keeping abreast of current issues and knowing how to let your voice be heard by decision makers, whether they are community leaders, national politicians, or business executives. Approaches to advocacy may include any of the following:

- attending government and community hearings and meetings
- calling, writing, or e-mailing elected representatives with your concerns and suggestions
- organizing a voter registration campaign for young and old
- sponsoring a parish, school, or community forum on political issues
- making families and parishioners aware of Catholic social teaching and current Church perspectives on important issues

A Trinity of Responses

Direct service, acts of justice, and words of advocacy offer a trinity of responses to today's pressing social needs. Taken together, they can help change the face of the earth and may even bring God's Kingdom a bit closer in our day. Young people have the talent and energy to join in this amazing adventure. At the end of this chapter, you will find a resource with a summary of key points about Justice, Service, and Advocacy from *Renewing the Vision*. To prepare leaders for justice and service, hand out this resource to your team members to read and discuss. Then you will be ready to use this manual to bring the justice journey to life for young people and to help them experience discipleship in action through justice, service, and advocacy for people in need.

Prayer for Peace and Justice

God, source of all light,
we are surrounded by the darkness of the injustices
experienced by your people:
the poor, who are hungry and who search for shelter,
the sick, who seek relief,
and the downtrodden, who seek help in their hopelessness.

Surround us, and fill us with your Spirit, who is Light.
Lead us in your way to be light to your people.
Help our parishes to be salt for the world
as we share your love with those caught in the struggles of life.

What Do You Think?

- How are you an advocate for young people whose voices are not heard?
- For whom could the young people advocate in your faith community?

We desire to be your presence to the least among us
and to know your presence in them as we work through you
to bring justice and peace to this world in desperate need.

We ask this through our Lord Jesus Christ, your Son,
who lives and reigns with you and the Holy Spirit,
one God, forever and ever.

Amen.

(USCCB, *Communities of Salt and Light Parish Resource Manual,* p. 52)

To Learn More

To learn more about justice, service, and advocacy, take a look at the following resources.

Books

- Daley, Shannon P., and Kathleen A. Guy. *Welcome the Child: A Child Advocacy Guide for Churches.* New York: Friendship Press, 1994.
- Massaro, Thomas J., and Thomas A. Shannon, editors. *American Catholic Social Teaching.* Collegeville, MN: The Liturgical Press, 2002.
- McKenna, Kevin E. *A Concise Guide to Catholic Social Teaching.* Notre Dame, IN: Ave Maria Press, 2002.
- O'Connell, Frances Hunt. *Giving and Growing* (Leader's Guide & Student Manual). Winona, MN: Saint Mary's Press, 1990.
- Search Institute. *Beyond Leaf-Raking.* Nashville, TN: Abingdon Press, 1993.

Church Documents

Summaries and excerpts are wonderful, but to appreciate the Church's social teaching, nothing is better than reading the documents themselves. Church documents can be long and heavy, but the latest justice resources from the U.S. bishops are fairly short and extremely reader-friendly. For a good sampling of social teaching, try the following:

- *A Place at the Table for All: A Catholic Commitment to Overcome Poverty and to Respect the Dignity of All God's Children* (2002) *www.usccb.org/bishops/table.htm*
- *Faithful Citizenship: Civic Responsibility for a New Millennium* (1999) *www.usccb.org/faithfulcitizenship/citizenship.htm*
- *In All Things Charity: A Pastoral Challenge for the New Millennium* (1999) *www.usccb.org/cchd/charity.htm*
- *Principles, Prophecy, and a Pastoral Response* (2002)
- *Putting Children and Families First: A Challenge for Our Church, Nation, and World* (1991)

- *Sharing Catholic Social Teaching: Challenges and Directions* (1999)
  www.usccb.org/sdwp/projects/socialteaching/socialteaching.htm

All these resources are available in print form from the USCCB Office of Publications. To order, visit the Web site at *www.usccb.org,* or call 800-235-8722.

Articles

St. Anthony Messenger Press offers a series of short updates in print and Web-based format on a variety of issues. Consider the following topics, then visit them online at *www.americancatholic.org.*

- "Facing Hunger in This Land of Plenty" (*Youth Update,* Y0102)
- "Faithful Citizenship: Bringing Moral Vision to Public Life" (*Catholic Update,* C0300)
- "God in Our Midst: Hungering for Justice" (*Everyday Catholic,* May 2002)
- "The Gospel of Life: An abbreviated version of Pope John Paul II's Pro-Life Encyclical" (*Catholic Update,* C0995)
- "JUBILEE 2000: How You Can Build a Better World" (*Catholic Update,* C0599)
- "Respect Life: The Bible and the Death Penalty Today" (*Scripture from Scratch,* N1000)

A Summary of Key Points from Renewing the Vision

About Advocacy

The ministry of advocacy engages the Church to examine its priorities and practices to determine how well young people are integrated into the life, mission, and work of the Catholic community.

Poor, vulnerable, and at-risk adolescents have first claim on our common efforts. The ministry of advocacy struggles against economic and social forces that threaten adolescents and family life.

We call upon all ministry leaders and faith communities to use the resources of our faith community, the gifts and talents of all our people, and the opportunities of this democracy to shape a society more respectful of the life, dignity, and rights of adolescents and their families.

The ministry of advocacy includes:
- affirming and protecting the sanctity of human life as a gift from God
- standing with and speaking on behalf of young people and their families
- empowering young people by giving them a voice and calling them to responsibility and accountability around the issues that affect them and their future . . .
- developing partnerships and initiatives with leaders and concerned citizens from all sectors of the community . . .

About Justice and Service

We are called as a Church to respond to people's present needs or crises, such as homelessness or hunger. We are also called to help change the policies, structures, and systems that perpetuate injustice, through legislative advocacy, community organizing, and work with social change organizations. Direct service needs to be coupled with action for justice so that adolescents experience the benefits of working directly with those in need and learn to change the systems that keeps people in need.

Justice and service with adolescents facilitate the following:

- engage young people in discovering the call to justice and service in the Scriptures, in the life of Jesus, and in Catholic social teaching;
- involve adolescents, their families, and parish communities in actions of direct service . . . and in efforts to address the causes of injustice and inequity;
- develop the assets, skills, and faith of young people by promoting gospel values in their lifestyles and choices . . .
- incorporate doing the right thing with attention to why and how we do what we do . . .
- involve a supportive community that . . . works together to serve and act for justice, and provide support and affirmation . . .
- nurture a lifelong commitment to service and justice involvement . . .

Justice and Service Sessions

2 A Catholic Approach to Justice and Service

AT A GLANCE

**Core Session:
A Catholic Approach
to Justice and Service
(55 minutes)**

- ◆ Involve: All I Really Need to Know . . .
  (5 minutes)
- ◆ Explore: Words of Community Wisdom
  (10 minutes)
- ◆ Reflect: Themes of Catholic Social Teaching
  (20 minutes)
- ◆ Act: Moving from Word to Witness
  (10 minutes)
- ◆ Pray: Voices of Hope and Challenge
  (10 minutes)

Overview

From its earliest days, the Church has been involved in serving people in need and speaking up for those whose needs go unheard. Beginning in 1891, the Church's teaching on the Christian call to justice and service has developed into a body of knowledge called Catholic social teaching. This session will help young people explore the wisdom found in the Church's social teaching and will examine how this teaching can be used to guide youth's involvement with people in need today. The session does not focus on a particular justice issue but, instead, provides participants with principles and approaches that can serve as building blocks for responding to any serious issue or concern.

Outcomes

- ◆ The participants will reflect on the beliefs and values that guide their interaction with others and their involvement with people in need.
- ◆ The participants will become familiar with the principal themes of Catholic social teaching and the direction the teaching provides for responding to today's social problems.
- ◆ The participants will be able to apply the principles of Catholic social teaching to issues of local concern.

Background Reading

- ◆ Scriptural connections: Obadiah, v. 15 (It shall be done to you.), Phil. 2:1–11 (imitating Christ), John 13:1–17 (Jesus washes the disciples' feet.)
- ◆ *Catholic Youth Bible* article connections: "Justice for Those Who Are Poor" (James 5:1–6), "Rethinking Social Structures" (Philem., vv. 8–21), "Jesus' Preference for the Poor" (Luke 6:17–49)

Core Session: A Catholic Approach to Justice and Service (55 minutes)

Preparation

- Gather the following items:
  - ❑ newsprint
  - ❑ markers, one for each small group of three or four
  - ❑ masking tape
  - ❑ blank writing paper or index cards
  - ❑ pens or pencils
  - ❑ basket
  - ❑ copies of handout 1, "The Major Themes of Catholic Social Teaching," one for each participant
  - ❑ three copies of resource 3, "Voices of Hope and Challenge," one for each reader
- Review resource 2, "All I Really Need to Know I Learned in Kindergarten." Select several learnings from the list of statements to share with your group. Be sure to include one or two that flow from a childhood story you are willing to share.
- Read through the relevant sections of *The Catholic Faith Handbook for Youth,* the *Catechism,* and *Sharing Catholic Social Teaching: Challenges and Directions—Reflections of the U.S. Catholic Bishops* (Washington, DC: United States Conference of Catholic Bishops, 1998, pp. 4–6). Be prepared to share the information with your group.
- Select an opening song.

Involve: All I Really Need To Know . . . (5 minutes)

1. Welcome participants, and provide them with a brief overview of today's session:

- Today we will be exploring the beliefs and values that influence how we relate to others and how we respond, particularly to people in need.
- I will begin with several quotes from a book published in the 1980s that was short in length but long on title. It is called *All I Really Need to Know I Learned in Kindergarten: Uncommon Thoughts on Common Things,* by Robert Fulghum (New York: Villard Books, 1988.)
- Listen closely as I read the excerpts; think about how the author's kindergarten experience matches yours.

Read the excerpts you have chosen to share.

2. After reading the quotes, offer a brief personal story on how your own learnings were similar to or different from Fulghum's. For example, you might focus on the sentence, "When you go out into the world, watch out for traffic, hold hands, and stick together." You could share how that helps you as an adult because you have learned how important teamwork is in getting a job done. Then invite the participants to share stories of their own—echoing Fulghum's lessons or adding learnings of their own to the mix. Post their responses on newsprint for all to see.

Explore: Words of Community Wisdom (10 minutes)

1. To introduce this section, say:
- As important as kindergarten may be, none of us actually started our learning there—or went from kindergarten to first grade having mastered everything needed for a full and happy life! We all left kindergarten with lots to learn, both in school and outside the traditional classroom.
- Let's take a look at words of wisdom we have since received from others.

2. Distribute index cards and pens or pencils to the participants, inviting them to spend a few minutes reflecting on the things they have learned outside the classroom about life. Provide them with these instructions:
- Identify someone—immediate family, close relative, good friend, someone from the local community whom you trust and respect—who has played an important part in shaping your life over the last few years. Write the person's name on the front of the index card.
- On the back of the index card, jot down a phrase or sentence that summarizes what that person taught you.

Allow a few minutes of reflection and writing time.

3. Invite the participants to share their writings, either in small groups or with the group as a whole. If the sharing is slow, begin with a story of your own. As an option, add these latest learnings to the newsprint list you started earlier.

4. Instruct participants to keep their pens or pencils. Collect their index cards for later use in prayer.

Reflect:
Themes of Catholic Social Teaching (20 minutes)

1. Review the progress you have made thus far in the session with these or similar comments:
- We heard Robert Fulghum's lessons from kindergarten, and we recalled what we have learned about life and love from our families, friends, and the people we trust and respect in our local community.
- Now we add a new element to the mix by looking at what the Church teaches us about what it means to live fully, honestly, and courageously as Christians.

2. Ask participants to answer these questions:

- Think about what the Church has to say about your relationships—with God, with others, and especially with the needy. What are those lessons?
- What lessons do you think the Church would add to the list already developed?
- Would the Church drop any of Fulghum's lessons from the list?
- Where do you think the Church places its strongest emphasis?

Invite participants' comments. Listen to what they have to say, avoiding any temptation to correct or amplify their thoughts.

3. Offer a brief presentation on a contemporary approach to Catholic social teaching. You will want to incorporate the following points into your presentation:

- From the earliest days of creation, people have been charged with the task of helping one another survive and flourish. Made in the image of God, human beings have been given the privilege and responsibility of reflecting God's love and compassion to others.
- In the Old Testament, God repeatedly raised up prophets as a reminder that the true measure of a peoples covenant relationship with God was how well they treated one another. God clearly listened to the cry of the poor.
- Jesus brought God's tradition of concern for the poor and vulnerable in the New Testament. In fact, the scene of the Last Judgment in Matthew's Gospel (25:31–46) demonstrates how deeply Jesus identifies with the poor and abandoned.
- Throughout time, the Church has continued Jesus' work of justice and service. As people of faith, we can be proud of this living tradition.
- In Jesus' name, the Church reaches out today to our brothers and sisters in need, providing food and shelter, guidance and education. It tries not to simply do things for the poor but to empower them to use their own gifts and talents to change the way things are.
- Beginning in the late 1800s, the Church began to consolidate its teaching on justice and service into a body of knowledge called Catholic social teaching. This teaching offers clear principles to guide us in the task of making Jesus' compassion known to all.
- To guide us in this direction, the Church offers the following seven principles, or themes:
  - Life and Dignity of the Human Person
  - Call to Family, Community, and Participation
  - Rights and Responsibilities of All People
  - Option for the Poor and Vulnerable
  - The Dignity of Work and the Rights of Workers
  - Solidarity
  - Care for God's Creation

4. Organize the participants into seven groups. Assign one of the Catholic social teaching themes to each group. Ask each group to come up with a simple definition of the theme and a two to three-sentence description of what the world would be like if the principle were fully accepted and lived out in our midst. For example, if the world practiced solidarity, we would not have wars, we would see one another as brothers and sisters. We would take care of mutual needs and focus on what we have in common, not what is different about us. There might not even be unfair import and export taxes, and racism might disappear too! Allow a few minutes for the groups to work through the assigned task.

5. Invite a representative from each group to come forward and share the insights into the Catholic social teaching theme they explored.

6. Next, distribute copies of handout 1, "The Major Themes of Catholic Social Teaching." Ask the participants to read the definitions and descriptions and to think about how these reflect and build on their group's insights. Ask them to discuss these questions:
- What makes the social teaching themes most attractive?
- What makes them most difficult to put into action today?

Act: Moving from Word to Witness (10 minutes)

1. Begin this final segment by reading the following quote:
- "Our faith calls us to work for justice; to serve those in need; to pursue peace; and to defend the life, dignity, and rights of all our sisters and brothers. This is the call of Jesus, the challenge of the prophets, and the living tradition of our Church." (United States Conference of Catholic Bishops, *A Century of Social Teaching*, p. 1)

Then make the following comments:
- This quote comes from another U.S. bishops' document, *A Century of Social Teaching*, and it challenges us to take the strong words we have just heard about justice and service and put them into action.
- The themes of Catholic social teaching are just empty words unless we take them to heart and move them into action, as individuals and as a society.

2. Invite participants to join you in exploring what it would look like to respond to an issue of local concern in a way that is consistent with the Church teaching they have just explored. Ask them:
- What social justice issues do you feel strongly about?

List their ideas on newsprint. Ask the participants to come to consensus about one issue they are most interested in studying further.

3. Organize the participants into groups of three or four, and distribute a sheet of newsprint and a marker to each group. Ask the groups to list as many options as they can for responding positively to the problem or concern that they have identified. To help them with this brainstorming activity, offer the following thoughts:

- Think about what you can do as *individuals and families*—and also as members of a *church, school, or community group.*
- Think creatively about ways to share not just what you own (possessions) but also your *talents and time.*
- Think about what needs to be done right now to assist with *immediate needs* (service) and what you can start doing to erase the *problem in the future* (advocacy).

Write the italicized words on a sheet of newsprint as you share them. Then post the newsprint where everyone can see it. Allow ample time for group discussion.

4. Invite group representatives to come forward to share their response lists. As they post their newsprint pages, comment briefly on the many different and creative approaches the groups have brainstormed.

5. Offer a brief summary of the session's learnings about Catholic social teaching and the direction it provides for moving from awareness of a need to an active response. Invite participants to comment about what they have learned and anything else that particularly struck them during the session.

Pray: Voices of Hope and Challenge (10 minutes)

Preparation

- Gather the following items:
  - ❑ a *Catholic Youth Bible* or other Bible
  - ❑ a cross
  - ❑ a pillar candle and matches
  - ❑ a basket
  - ❑ seasonal decorations
- Establish a prayer center in the space you will be using for this session. Cover a small table with a colorful cloth. Arrange a Bible, a cross, a candle, a basket, and any seasonal decoration you deem appropriate on the table. Allow enough space around the table for participants to gather comfortably for prayer.
- Recruit four participants as readers. Provide them with the readings.

1. Invite participants to gather in silence around the prayer table. Then invite them to join in singing the opening song you have chosen.

Spirit & Song
connections

- "The Cry of the Poor," by John Foley, SJ
- "The Summons," by John L. Bell

2. Place the index cards developed during the opening activity into the basket. Raise the basket so everyone can see it. Ask the participants to join you in a silent prayer of thanksgiving for the family, friends, and community members who have helped shape their beliefs and values. After a moment's silence, say:

- Ever-present and ever-loving God, we thank you for your care for us and for all of creation. We thank you for all those who have been a sign of your love in our lives. We ask for strength so that we can join Jesus in responding to the needs of people around us today. We ask this in the name of the Father and of the Son and of the Holy Spirit. Amen.

3. Invite the first reader to come forward and proclaim Luke 4:14–21. Allow a few moments for silent reflection. Ask the participants to reflect quietly on this question:

- How has God sent you "to bring good news to the poor"?

4. Invite the second reader to read the quote from Mother Teresa found on resource 3, "Voices of Hope and Challenge." Ask the participants to quietly reflect on this question:

- What can the poor teach me about Jesus' unconditional love?

5. Invite the third reader to read the quote from the Maryknoll Fathers and Brothers found on resource 3. Ask the participants to quietly reflect on this question:

- How does Jesus use me to be a healing presence in the world?

6. Invite the fourth reader to read the quote from Dorothy Day found on resource 3. Ask the participants to quietly reflect on this question:

- How will I respond the next time I encounter a poor or homeless person?

7. Invite participants to share a prayer of petition for a need they would like to raise. Use "Lord, help us be disciples of justice and service" as the response.

8. Thank the participants for their openness in listening and responding to God's call to justice and service. Invite them to offer one another a sign of peace. Conclude by inviting the participants to join in singing a closing song.

All I Really Need to Know I Learned in Kindergarten

ALL I REALLY NEED TO KNOW about how to live and what to do and how to be I learned in kindergarten. Wisdom was not at the top of the graduate-school mountain, but there in the sandpile at Sunday School. These are the things I learned:

Share everything.

Play fair.

Don't hit people.

Put things back where you found them.

Clean up your own mess.

Don't take things that aren't yours.

Say you're sorry when you hurt somebody.

Wash your hands before you eat.

Flush.

Warm cookies and cold milk are good for you.

Live a balanced life—learn some and think some and draw and paint and sing and dance and play and work every day some.

Take a nap every afternoon.

When you go out into the world, watch out for traffic, hold hands, and stick together.

Be aware of wonder. Remember the little seed in the Styrofoam cup: the roots go down and the plant goes up and nobody really knows how or why, but we are all like that.

Goldfish and hamsters and white mice and even the little seed in the Styrofoam cup—they all die. So do we.

And then remember the Dick-and-Jane books and the first word you learned—the biggest word of all—LOOK.

Everything you need to know is in there somewhere. The Golden Rule and love and basic sanitation. Ecology and politics and equality and sane living.

Take any of those items and extrapolate it into sophisticated adult terms and apply it to your family life or your work or your government or your world and it holds true and clear and firm. Think what a better world it would be if we all—the whole world—had cookies and milk about three o'clock every afternoon and then lay down with our blankets for a nap. Or if all governments had as a basic policy to always put things back where they found them and to clean up their own mess.

And it is still true, no matter how old you are—when you go out into the world, it is best to hold hands and stick together.

(This resource is excerpted from *All I Really Need to Know I Learned in Kindergarten: Uncommon Thoughts on Common Things*, by Robert L. Fulghum [New York: Villard Books, 1988], pages 6–8. Copyright © 1986, 1988 by Robert L. Fulghum. Used with permission of Villard Books, a division of Random House, Inc.)

The Major Themes of Catholic Social Teaching

The Church's social teaching is a rich treasure of wisdom about building a just society and living lives of holiness amid the challenges of modern society. . . . Modern Catholic social teaching has been articulated through a tradition of papal, conciliar, and episcopal documents. . . . The depth and richness of this tradition can be understood best through a direct reading of these documents. . . . In these brief reflections, we wish to highlight several of the key themes that are at the heart of our Catholic social tradition.

Life and Dignity of the Human Person

The Catholic Church proclaims that human life is sacred and that the dignity of the human person is the foundation of a moral vision for society. Our belief in the sanctity of human life and the inherent dignity of the human person is the foundation of all the principles of our social teaching. In our society, human life is under direct attack from abortion and assisted suicide. The value of human life is being threatened by increasing use of the death penalty. We believe that every person is precious, that people are more important than things, and that the measure of every institution is whether it threatens or enhances the life and dignity of the human person.

Call to Family, Community, and Participation

The person is not only sacred but also social. How we organize our society—in economics and politics, in law and policy—directly affects human dignity and the capacity of individuals to grow in community. The family is the central social institu-tion that must be supported and strengthened, not undermined. We believe people have a right and a duty to participate in society, seeking together the common good and well-being of all, especially the poor and vulnerable.

Rights and Responsibilities of All People

The Catholic tradition teaches that human dignity can be protected and a healthy community can be achieved only if human rights are protected and responsibilities are met. Therefore, every person has a fundamental right to life and a right to those things required for human decency. Corresponding to these rights are duties and responsibilities—to one another, to our families, and to the larger society.

Option for the Poor and Vulnerable

A basic moral test is how our most vulnerable members are faring. In a society marred by deepening divisions between rich and poor, our tradition recalls the story of the Last Judgment (Matthew 25:31–46) and instructs us to put the needs of the poor and vulnerable first.

The Dignity of Work and the Rights of Workers

The economy must serve people, not the other way around. Work is more than a way to make a living; it is a form of continuing participation in God's creation. If the dignity of work is to be protected, the basic rights of workers must be respected—the right to productive work, to decent and fair wages, to organize and join unions, to private property, and to economic initiative.

Solidarity

We are our brothers' and sisters' keepers, wherever they live. We are one human family, whatever our national, racial, ethnic, economic, and ideological differences. Learning to practice the virtue of solidarity means learning that "loving our neighbor" has global dimensions in an interdependent world.

Care for God's Creation

We show our respect for the Creator by our stewardship of creation. Care for the earth is not just an Earth Day slogan; it is a requirement of our faith. We are called to protect people and the planet, living our faith in relationship with all of God's creation. This environmental challenge has fundamental moral and ethical dimensions that cannot be ignored.

Voices of Hope and Challenge

Mother Teresa

"The poor are great. We have to love them, but not with pity love. We have to love them because it is Jesus who hides under the likeness of the poor. They are our brothers and sisters. They belong to us. The lepers, the dying, the starving, the naked—all of them are Jesus." (from *Heart of Joy,* by Mother Teresa (Ann Arbor, MI: Servant Publications, 1987), page 6. Copyright © 1987 by José Luis Gonzalez-Balado. Published by Servant Publications, Box 8617, Ann Arbor MI 48107. Used with permission.)

Maryknoll Fathers and Brothers

"We join the struggles for justice of the poor, indigenous peoples, women and children against economic, social, and cultural oppression. Everywhere we are touched by the triumph of the human spirit and enriched by encountering people's faith and experience. We join with them announcing the healing, reconciling, and liberating Jesus." ("Mission Vision Statement," in *Maryknoll Magazine,* February 2003, at *www.mary knoll.org/MEDIA/x/MAGAZINE/xmag2003/xmag02/m2s2.htm.* Used with permission.)

Dorothy Day

"The mystery of the poor is this: that they are Jesus, and what you do for them you do for Him. It is the only way we have of knowing and believing in our love. The mystery of poverty is that by sharing in it, making ourselves poor in giving to others, we increase our knowledge of and belief in love." (*The Catholic Worker,* April 1964.)

**Core Session:
Life:
Who Gets
to Choose?**
(50 minutes)

◆ Involve: Who Deserves
the Death Penalty?
(10 minutes)

◆ Explore: Analyzing
the "Why"
(10 minutes)

◆ Reflect: Consistent
Ethic of Life
(10 minutes)

◆ Act: Choosing a Life Issue
to Protect
(10 minutes)

◆ Pray: Prayer for Mercy
(10 minutes)

3
Life:
Who Gets to Choose?

Overview

While society often takes a "pick and choose" attitude toward life issues, the Catholic Church insists on the consistent ethic of life. This session engages youth in examining their opinions and feelings about a particular life issue—the death penalty—then puts them in dialogue with the Church's seamless-garment approach to all life issues.

Outcomes

◆ The participants will examine their own beliefs about the death penalty and the reasons why they believe as they do.

◆ The participants will understand what the Catholic Church teaches about the death penalty and other life issues under the consistent ethic of life.

◆ The participants will reexamine their own beliefs about life issues in light of what the Church teaches and will choose their own action to promote life.

Background Reading

◆ Scriptural connections: Exod. 1:15–22 (right to life), Matt. 5:43–48 (love for enemies)

◆ *Catholic Youth Bible* article connections: "The Sacredness of Life" (Psalm 139), "The Slaughter of the Innocents" (Matt. 2:16–18), "The Cycle of Violence" (Gen. 4:15)

Core Session:
Life: Who Gets to Choose?
(50 minutes)

Preparation

- Gather the following items:
  - ❑ index cards, one blue and one pink for each participant
  - ❑ pens or pencils
  - ❑ newsprint
  - ❑ markers
  - ❑ a *Catholic Youth Bible* or other Bible
  - ❑ copies of handout 2, "Who Deserves the Death Penalty?," one for each participant
  - ❑ copies of resource 4, "Choosing a Life Issue to Protect," one for each small group leader
  - ❑ copies of the song "Prayer of Saint Francis" or another song with the dignity of persons as its theme, one for each participant
  - ❑ materials for a prayer center, including a cloth, a *Catholic Youth Bible* or other Bible, a cross, a large candle, matches, and a statue of the hand of God cradling a person (optional)
- Prepare two cloths, one from a single piece of fabric with the quote "Every person is created in God's own image" written on it with a fine-line permanent marker. The second cloth should be made from several small pieces of fabric sewn loosely together, each piece having one of the following phrases written on it:
  - ○ an unborn baby
  - ○ a prisoner on death row
  - ○ a person dying of bone cancer
  - ○ a civilian in a country that protects terrorists
  - ○ an elderly person

Involve: Who Deserves the Death Penalty? (10 minutes)

1. Welcome participants, and provide an overview of the session. Distribute a pink and a blue index card to each participant. Explain the activity as follows:

- I will be reading several descriptions of people who have committed very serious crimes. Raise your pink card if you think the person deserves the death penalty. Raise your blue card if you think the person does not deserve the death penalty.

Read the following descriptions aloud, giving participants enough time to raise their index cards in response to each statement.

- A cult leader sends his followers to the home of a woman who is eight months pregnant. He has ordered the cult members to kill her and everyone else in her home, which they do. He shows no remorse, but he did not actually commit the murders himself.
- A man trains terrorists and sends them on suicide attacks that kill thousands of innocent people in an "enemy" country.
- A thief is caught by police in the act of robbing a convenience store. The thief grabs his gun and kills a female police officer, who is the mother of two small children.
- A mentally challenged 18-year-old kills a woman who caught him robbing her home.
- A father kills a drug dealer who sold crack to his 13-year-old son.
- A woman participates in a very vicious murder, committed with an ax, but admits her crime and professes her repentance, asking forgiveness of God and the victim's family.
- A pedophile kidnaps, rapes, and then murders a 10-year-old girl.
- Two brothers, ages 12 and 14, beat their father to death with a baseball bat. He had abused them physically and emotionally for many years.

Explore: Analyzing the "Why" (10 minutes)

1. Tell participants they are now going to analyze their own motives for making the choices they did in the previous exercise. Distribute copies of handout 2, "Who Deserves the Death Penalty?" and a pen or pencil to each participant. Give these instructions:

- Quietly complete the handout by identifying the criteria you used to decide who deserved or did not deserve the death penalty.
- You have four choices for each item: (1) it significantly influenced your decision; (2) it influenced you somewhat; or (3) it hardly influenced you; or (4) did not influence you at all.

Give the participants several minutes to write their individual responses on the handout.

2. Organize the participants into small groups of five or six. Invite them to share the significant influences on their decisions with their group. Ask them to keep track of any items that were significant for all or most of the group members. Ask one person from each small group to share with the large group the most significant influences they identified. Post these on newsprint or on the board.

3. In the large group, ask the following:

- What do a death row inmate and an unborn baby have in common?

Post their responses on newsprint. After you receive several responses, ask:

- What do an unborn baby and a person dying a slow and painful death from a terminal disease have in common?

Again, allow for several responses. Then ask:

- What do a person dying painfully and a Jew in Nazi Germany have in common?

Again, allow for several responses. Finally, ask:

- What do a Jewish person in Nazi Germany and an innocent civilian who dies from a bomb dropped on her village during a war have in common?

When you have received several responses, ask the participants to identify the common thread among all four pairs of people mentioned. Look for the points that they are all human persons, all created in God's image, all people whose lives are in jeopardy.

Reflect: Consistent Ethic of Life (10 minutes)

1. Give a short presentation on the Church's position on life issues. Be sure to highlight the following points:

- Our Church teaches that every human life is sacred because we are all created in the image and likeness of God. Because we are made in God's image, we all have a dignity and a worth that can never be taken away.
- We are responsible for protecting the dignity of all, even people who have killed someone else.
- John Paul II, in his encyclical *The Gospel of Life,* talks specifically about capital punishment in paragraph 57. He says that executing someone for a crime is an extreme measure that should happen only when absolutely necessary. Given today's prison systems, the pope says, such a situation is rare, if not nonexistent.
- For Catholics, being pro-life means defending the dignity of all human life, from unborn babies to people at the end of their life. This dignity is not based on what we do or do not do, what we "deserve" or don't deserve. It is based on one fact alone—all of us are created in God's own image and likeness. We call this position the *consistent ethic of life,* or the *seamless-garment* approach to life.

2. Using the first piece of cloth you have prepared (the one inscribed with "Every person is created in God's own image"), ask two volunteers to come forward and hold the piece of cloth in their hands. Challenge them to tear the cloth apart while holding it in both hands. After they have tried and failed, give them the second piece of cloth, made up of several smaller pieces. Make sure the participants can read the various phrases written on the pieces. Invite the two volunteers to grasp the cloth with both hands and try to tear it. Because it is vulnerable at the seams, the cloth will come apart rather easily.

3. Ask the participants what they think the point of this demonstration is. Draw out of them—and reiterate—the following points:

- A great gift of the Catholic Church's position on life, then, is its consistency. We never have to guess who deserves to live and who deserves to die. Only God has the wisdom, the big picture, and the penetrating view of each human heart to do this.
- When Mother Teresa gave her acceptance speech for the Nobel Peace Prize, she spoke out against abortion. "And this is what is the greatest destroyer of peace today. Because if a mother can kill her own child, what is left for me to kill you and you to kill me? There is nothing between." (Mother Teresa, Nobel Peace Prize acceptance speech in 1979, *www.tisv. be/mt/en/nobel.htm.*) It is interesting that her predictions are coming true in some states of our own country, as well as in countries around the world, which first tolerated abortion and now allow for assisted suicide.

4. Summarize the seamless-garment approach by concluding with this explanation:

- When Cardinal Joseph Bernardin (former cardinal of the Archdiocese of Chicago) was alive, he cared passionately about preserving the sacredness of all life—from womb to tomb. He is the person who first used the concept of the seamless-garment approach to life. (See *A Consistent Ethic of Life: Continuing the Dialogue,* by Joseph Cardinal Bernardin, at The William Wade Lecture Series, Saint Louis University, March 11, 1984.)
- Cardinal Bernardin based this concept of a seamless garment on a quote from the Gospel of John: "When the soldiers had crucified Jesus, they took his clothes and divided them into four parts, one for each soldier. They also took his tunic; now the tunic was seamless, woven in one piece from the top. So they said to one another, 'Let us not tear it, but cast lots for it to see who will get it.' This was to fulfill what the scripture says, 'They divided my clothes among themselves, and for my clothing they cast lots.'" (John 19:23–24)

Act: Choosing a Life Issue to Protect (10 minutes)

1. Ask the participants to brainstorm which life issues are most violated in their local community, their state, and in the United States. Post their answers on newsprint.

2. Organize the participants into interest groups (abortion, the death penalty, assisted suicide, or other life issues they identify). Ask each group to respond to the following question:

- What can you do to preserve life in each threatened group?

If a group struggles to find ideas, provide a copy of resource 4, "Choosing a Life Issue to Protect."

3. Once the groups have had several minutes to come up with ideas, invite individual participants to share what they plan to do to take a stand for life.

Pray: Prayer for Mercy (10 minutes)

Preparation

- Gather the following items:
  - ❑ a cloth
  - ❑ a *Catholic Youth Bible* or other Bible
  - ❑ a cross
  - ❑ a pillar candle and matches
  - ❑ a statue of the hand of God cradling a person (optional)
  - ❑ copies of the song "Prayer of Saint Francis" or another song with the dignity of persons as its theme, one for each participant
- Establish a prayer center in the space you will be using for this session. Cover a small table with a colorful cloth. Arrange a Bible, a cross, and a candle on the table. If possible, include a statue of the hand of God cradling a person.
- Recruit a reader to proclaim John 10:9–10.

1. Gather participants together around the prayer table. Encourage them to spend a few minutes in silence as they gather their thoughts about the life issues you have discussed. Remind them of the presence of God, a God who loves each one of them unconditionally.

2. Invite the participants to join in singing the "Prayer of Saint Francis" or the alternate gathering song you have chosen.

3. Invite the reader to come forward and proclaim John 10:9–10. Allow a few moments for quiet reflection.

4. Invite the participants to share a petition based on something they have learned in the session or something they want to do to support life in the future. Ask all participants to respond to each petition with "Lord, help us to be merciful."

5. Conclude the prayer by praying together the Lord's Prayer, inviting participants to focus especially on the line "forgive us our trespasses as we forgive those who trespass against us."

Spirit & Song connections

- "My Life Is in Your Hands," by Kathy Troccoli and Bill Montvilo
- "Prayer of St. Francis," by Sebastian Temple
- "The Lord Is Kind and Merciful," by Rick Modlin

Mediaconnections

- Check out the video *Death No More: A Look at the Death Penalty* (Brown-ROA Publishing, 1999, 40 minutes), which includes an interview with Sister Helen Prejean.
- Consider the resources provided by these Web sites:
  - ◇ *www.deathpenaltyinfo.org* (Death Penalty Information Center)
  - ◇ *www.cacp.org* (Catholics Against Capital Punishment)
  - ◇ *www.ncadp.org* (National Coalition to Abolish the Death Penalty)

Who Deserves the Death Penalty?

Check whether each of the following factors influenced you significantly, somewhat, hardly, or not at all in choosing life or death for each criminal.

About the Murderer	Significantly	Somewhat	Hardly	Not at All
The murderer's reason for killing	☐	☐	☐	☐
The age of the murderer	☐	☐	☐	☐
The upbringing of the murderer	☐	☐	☐	☐
Whether or not the murderer was sorry	☐	☐	☐	☐
Whether the murderer fully understood what he or she was doing	☐	☐	☐	☐

About the Victim	Significantly	Somewhat	Hardly	Not at All
How innocent the victim is	☐	☐	☐	☐
How old the victim is	☐	☐	☐	☐
How much the victim contributes to society	☐	☐	☐	☐
How much the victim suffers	☐	☐	☐	☐
How many others are affected by the victim's death	☐	☐	☐	☐

About Me	Significantly	Somewhat	Hardly	Not at All
What my conscience says	☐	☐	☐	☐
What my family and friends say	☐	☐	☐	☐
What society says	☐	☐	☐	☐
What my faith says	☐	☐	☐	☐

What other factors influenced your decision?

Choosing a Life Issue to Protect

If your small group is having difficulty coming up with ideas on how to help protect a life issue, use the following suggestions to get the conversation started.

Abortion

- Support the local pro-life organization with a fund-raiser or by offering your time.
- Plan and implement a baby shower for a local emergency pregnancy service that does not endorse abortion.
- Find out which U.S. Supreme Court justices support abortion. Call the White House hotline (202-456-1111) to express your support of the President's nominating pro-life candidates to the Court.
- Make a commitment to pray every day for the baby who is in the most immediate danger of being aborted.
- Organize a public prayer service or silent vigil near an abortion clinic.
- Consider holding the prayer service on or near January 22, the date in 1973 when *Roe v. Wade* made abortion legal in the United States.

Capital Punishment

- Write a letter to the state legislature if you live in a state that has the death penalty. In the letter, share your feelings about the death penalty and why you think the law needs to be changed.
- Write a letter to a person on death row, offering your prayers. Contact your Diocesan Prison Ministry or Social Justice office to learn how to contact someone on death row.
- Create a card to keep in your wallet, explaining that if you are killed by a violent crime, you do not want your attacker to receive the death penalty.

Assisted Suicide

- Write to your state legislature, expressing your disapproval of any law that allows for assisted suicide or euthanasia.
- E-mail your Congressional representatives to let them know your feelings about legalizing assisted suicide.
- Support a local hospice organization through a fund-raiser or volunteer hours.

Children's Rights:
National, Global, and Galactic

Overview

Sadly, the rights of children and youth are still to be fully realized in our country and in our world. Too many children suffer from the lack of life's essentials and go without the protection needed to grow in body, mind, and spirit. This session helps participants explore the meaning of children's rights and apply what they learn from international conventions and the wisdom of the Church to the situation of children in need. The session offers advocacy as an approach to justice and provides multiple options for extending action beyond the core session.

Outcomes

◆ The participants will identify and empathize with the poor and needy children of the world.

◆ The participants will be able to explain the threefold rights of children as laid out in the United Nations' *Convention on the Rights of the Child*—provision, protection, and participation.

◆ The participants will undertake advocacy for the rights of children and families in need as an expression of the Christian call to justice and solidarity.

Background Reading

◆ Scriptural connections: Micah 6:8 (Do justice, love kindness, walk humbly.), Isa. 58:6–14 (Loosen the bonds of injustice.)

◆ *Catholic Youth Bible* article connections: "What Goes Around" (Obad., v. 15), "Stand Up and Be Counted" (Amos 8:4–8), "I Therefore Commit" (Hos. 12:2–6)

Core Session:
Children's Rights: National, Global, and Galactic (55 minutes)

Preparation

- Gather the following items:
  - ❑ *Catholic Youth Bibles* or other Bibles, for selected readers or all participants
  - ❑ newsprint
  - ❑ markers
  - ❑ masking tape
  - ❑ pens or pencils
  - ❑ copies of handout 3, "Children and the Three P's," one for each participant
  - ❑ copies of handout 4, "Prayer Through the Eyes of a Child in Need," one for each participant
- Read through the talk points on the United Nations' *Convention on the Rights of the Child (www.unhchr.ch/html/menu3/b/k2crc.htm),* and be prepared to provide a short presentation.
- Cut out pictures from magazines (such as *National Geographic, Maryknoll Magazine,* and so forth) of children from around the world. You will need one picture for every two participants. Place these pictures on the prayer table.
- Select a gathering and a closing song with the theme of taking care of the defenseless, the young, and the vulnerable.

Involve: A New Generation of Colonists (20 minutes)

1. Organize participants into teams of four to six. Ask them to listen closely as you read through the following scenario.

- The year is 2025. For the first time in recorded history, the nations of the world are universally at peace. The wars of the past are fading in memory, and a spirit of hope and optimism prevails.
- The world's military spending is just a fraction of what it was. The resources once allotted to defense are now spent on health and education, science and art. Countries are healing one another's hurts and responding to one another's needs. The wealthy continue to have all they want, and the number of people living in poverty is on the decline and promises to disappear entirely by the decade's end. Not everything is perfect, but life looks better than it has in centuries.

- You are an adult in your early 30s. Like almost everyone, you have benefited from the change in the world's condition. Science has been your passion since you were young, and you are now headed into an adventure that scientists of all time would envy.

- Along with 200 other people, you are on your way to establish Earth's first space colony. You know the future holds countless challenges, but there is no place else you would rather be. The task at hand is to use the travel time to prepare for the challenges of the future. There is learning to be done, work to be accomplished and, most importantly, a new community to be shaped and formed.

- Nothing will succeed unless all the colonists are of one heart and mind about the truly important things in life. Your fellow colonists are a diverse lot in age and ethnicity, language and tradition, experience and education, but all are committed to working together to avoid the mistakes of the world you have left behind.

- Your new community has been given the task of creating an intergalactic statement on the rights of children. How do you define the word "child"? How will your children live? What do they have a right to expect from you and from this new society?

- What rights will you guarantee for all your children, regardless of who their parents are or where they were born?

- Your resources—material and human—are limited, and you know you will not be able to respond to all of your children's whims and wants, but you will try to meet every legitimate need. You know that your new colony will not grow and thrive unless its children do.

- Your task is to develop together, in outline form, a new "Charter on the Rights of the Galaxy's Children."

Check to make sure everyone understands the task, and clarify any questions the participants might have. Then provide each group with a few sheets of newsprint and several markers. Allow about 10 minutes for discussion and group work.

2. Ask the groups to post their newsprint on the walls around the room. Invite the participants to walk around the room for a few minutes to check out one another's charter statements. Then ask the participants the following questions:

- What similarities do you see in the statements?
- What differences are there?
- What rights, if any, are universally accepted?

Explore: Guaranteeing the Three P's (10 minutes)

1. Tell the participants that although we have not yet, as a society, created a galactic statement on children's rights, the United Nations has promulgated the *International Convention on the Rights of the Child.* Most of the nations of the world have signed on to the *Convention,* including the Vatican state, which was among the first to sign. Provide a brief overview of the *Convention,* including the following points:

- *The Convention on the Rights of the Child* is a human rights treaty approved by the United Nations General Assembly in 1989.
- The *Convention* establishes shared norms and standards nations can use to develop and evaluate their programs on behalf of children.
- The *Convention* calls for governments to respect the rights, responsibilities, and duties of parents—and encourages governments to support families in raising their children in an environment of love, happiness, and understanding.
- The *Convention* promotes international norms that guarantee children equal treatment regardless of their gender, race, or cultural background, and promotes a positive response to their needs.
- The basic children's rights laid out in the *Convention* can be categorized under the three P's—Provision, Protection, and Participation:
  - Provision—Providing children with the essential goods and services they need to grow and develop, including food and shelter, health care, education, rest and play, and special care for disabled or parentless children.
  - Protection—Protecting children from harmful acts or practices that prevent their full growth, such as forced separation from parents or family, commercial or sexual exploitation, physical or sexual abuse, and involvement in warfare.
  - Participation—Involving children in decision making on issues that impact their lives. As they grow from infants to adolescents, children should have increased opportunities to influence the decisions made about them and the communities in which they live.

2. Following your presentation, ask the participants to gather back into their small groups. Provide each group with a copy of handout 3, "Children and the Three P's." Give these instructions:

- Review the rights listed in your group's charter, and transfer them onto the handout, using the categories of provision, protection, and participation as your guide.

Allow a few minutes for them to complete this task. Then say:

- In your groups, discuss which category was strongest in your charter, and which was weakest. What two or three things do you think you should add to your list of rights after learning about the United Nations *Convention?*

After a few minutes, invite the teams to share what they learned.

TryThis

The *Convention on the Rights of the Child* is the most widely, and rapidly ratified human rights treaty in history. Of the United Nations' 193 participating nations, only 2 have yet to ratify the document: Somalia (which, as of June 2003, still has no officially recognized government) and the United States of America. To better understand the reasons for the delay in U.S. ratification of the *Convention,* check the Web site of the United States Fund for UNICEF: *www.unicefusa. org.*

TryThis

◆ Invite the participants to take their first step in advocacy by writing and signing their names to a simple statement that reflects their concern about the absence of children's rights in parts of their nation or world. Once completed, this statement can be shared with their families and with the wider parish community.

◆ Suggest that participants take a second step on their own during the week by keeping a log of how the news media handles children's issues. How often are the rights of children explicitly mentioned? Are social issues covered in a way that gives appropriate weight to children's rights?

Reflect:
Putting Children and Families First (5 minutes)

1. Ask for volunteers to read the Gospel passages: Matt. 19:12–15 and Mark 9:36–37. Allow a few moments for quiet reflection. Then say:

• It is clear from these stories that Jesus stands for the dignity of children and is not happy when they are pushed aside or considered of little worth. As a faithful Jew and as God's Son, Jesus shows an ever-present concern and compassion for those who are poor and helpless in the world—and children too frequently fall into this category.

• The Church continues Jesus' tradition of caring for infants and young children, for pre-teens and teens, and for families. This is evident over the centuries in the different ministries founded by the Church. It is evident, as well, in the Church's teaching on justice and service.

• In 1992 the U.S. bishops wrote a special letter on the situation of children and families in need. The letter was titled *Putting Children and Families First: A Challenge for Our Church, Nation, and the World.* The challenge raised in the bishops' letter of "reordering of priorities . . . to focus more on the needs and potential of our children" remains an issue today and calls for a response from all followers of Christ (United States Conference of Catholic Bishops, *Putting Children and Families First*, p. 1).

Act: Taking a Stand for Children's Rights (10 minutes)

1. Say to the participants:

• Now that we have viewed how two large and influential international organizations—the United Nations and the Roman Catholic Church—view children's roles and rights, it is a good time to look at how we are doing as a society in respecting the dignity and meeting the needs of children.

2. Post two sheets of newsprint. On one, write "In the United States." On the other, write "In Our World." Invite participants to think about how far they think we have come as a world community in guaranteeing the rights of all children. Tell them you will briefly record their responses to the following questions on the appropriate newsprint sheet. Ask participants to offer examples or reasons to support their beliefs.

• As you look at the big picture—how children are treated in our country and in the world at large—how far do you think we have come in meeting their legitimate needs?

• Where is respect for children's rights most evident? most lacking?

• Which rights of children do you think are most often set aside in the United States? in the world at large?

- How well are we doing in meeting the requirements of provision—meeting children's most basic needs?
- How well are we doing in protection—sheltering children from abuse, neglect, and exploitation?
- How are we doing by way of participation—calling children and youth to involvement in the important decisions that will affect their lives?

After a few minutes, invite the participants to offer summarizing statements on what they see noted on the newsprint sheets before them. For example, they may recognize that they are unaware of the way children are treated nationally and/or globally.

3. Suggest that different problems and needs require different responses. Include these or similar comments:

- Given the size and scope of the problems we have talked about during the session, an approach called advocacy may be the best way to go.
- When you hear the word advocacy, what comes to mind?

Elicit a few suggestions from the participants. Then build on their ideas with the following description:

- Advocacy is about standing with and speaking on behalf of people whose dignity and/or rights are pushed aside or denied. People who are advocates make others aware of the issue and join with them to change the situation.
- Advocacy often promotes people's active involvement in the political and economic spheres. It gets people working together for the common good.

Pray: Through the Eyes of a Child in Need (10 minutes)

Preparation

- Gather the following items:
  - ❑ a cloth
  - ❑ a *Catholic Youth Bible* or other Bible
  - ❑ a pillar candle and matches
  - ❑ items related to children, such as a storybook, a small toy, child-size shoes, or a baby blanket, and pictures of children from around the world
- Establish a prayer center in the space you will be using for this session. Cover a small table with a cloth. Arrange a Bible, a cross, a candle, and a few items related to children, such as a storybook, a small toy, child-size shoes, or a baby blanket on the table. Put the prayer center where it will be visible during the session, allowing enough space around the table for participants to gather comfortably for prayer.
- Recruit a reader to proclaim Psalm 144 in the closing prayer.

Spirit & Song connections

- "Malo! Malo! Thanks Be to God," by Jesse Manibusan
- "Power of Peace," by Jesse Manibusan
- "With One Voice," by Ricky Manalo

Mediaconnections

- Check out the Voices for Youth Web site, a worldwide, electronic discussion forum for children and young people located at *www.unicef.org.*

◆ UNICEF offers a variety of videos that address the session topics. Access information about them at: *www.unicefusa.org/educa tion/video.html.* One such video is:
◇ *Raised Voices* (1993, 30 minutes). In this compelling documentary, children and teenagers talk about issues that concern them and how they can act to change the future.
◆ Additional Web sites you might find useful include:
◇ Children's Defense Fund *(www.childrens defense.org)*
◇ National Center for Children in Poverty *(www.nccp.org)*
◇ Kids Count *(www.aecf.org)*
◇ Stand for Children *(www.stand.org)*
◇ National Association of Child Advocates *(www.childadvocacy.org)*

1. Gather the participants around the prayer table. Distribute handout 4, "Prayer Through the Eyes of a Child in Need," to each participant. Invite the participants to choose a prayer partner. Give this instruction:

• With your prayer partner, select a picture of a child from the prayer table. When you have made your selection, be seated.

2. Invite the reader to come forward and proclaim Ps. 144.

3. Invite the participants to join in singing the gathering song you have chosen.

4. Invite the participants to reflect on the picture of a child that they selected. Ask them to develop a prayer of intercession for the child in the photograph. Allow a few minutes for them to create their prayer.

5. Invite each set of participants to offer their prayer of intercession inviting all to respond to each prayer with "Lord, bring life and healing to all your children."

6. Together, pray the prayer on handout 4, "Prayer Through the Eyes of a Child in Need."

7. Invite the participants to extend to one another a sign of God's peace. End the session by inviting them to sing the closing song you have selected.

Children and the Three P's

Review the rights listed in your group's charter. Transfer these rights to this worksheet, using the categories of provision, protection, and participation as your guide.

Provision: Providing the goods and services children need to grow and develop.
Examples: food, shelter, health care, education, rest, play, care for orphans and persons with disabilities.

Protection: Protecting children from harmful acts and practices.
Examples: forced separation from family, exploitation, abuse, and involvement in war.

Participation: Increasing the involvement of children in the decisions that impact their lives. Examples: education and work choices, family custody decisions, political and religious participation.

Which of the above categories was strongest in your charter? Which was weakest?

Which two or three additions would help bring your charter into better alignment with the United Nations' document?

Prayer Through the Eyes of a Child in Need

Reader: They tell me, and I believe, God, that you are the Way.

All: *When I feel lost and alone, be there as my Guide.*

Reader: They tell me, and I believe, God, that you are Love.

All: *When I think no one cares or holds me precious in their sight, fold me close in your loving embrace.*

Reader: They tell me, and I believe, God, that you are Light.

All: *When my dignity is denied and prejudice rules over reason, reveal the goodness of all you have made.*

Reader: They tell me, and I believe, God, that you are the Bread of Life.

All: *When my stomach is empty or my growth put at risk, provide what I lack and a little to share.*

Reader: They tell me, and I believe, God, that you are the Water of Life.

All: *When I thirst for drink or companionship, quench my need.*

Reader: They tell me, and I believe, God, that you are Truth.

All: *When I am confused and lose the sense of what is right, tell me again what you want for me and for the world. I ask this with confidence in the Name of the Father and of the Son and of the Holy Spirit. Amen.*

5 Exactly What Is a Just Wage?

AT A GLANCE

Core Session: Exactly What Is a Just Wage? (60 minutes)

- ◆ Involve: What We Have (20 minutes)
- ◆ Explore: Presenting Poverty (10 minutes)
- ◆ Reflect: The Church on Wages (10 minutes)
- ◆ Act: Take Action (10 minutes)
- ◆ Pray: Prayer for Workers (10 minutes)

Overview

It is a common misconception that if poor people would just work, they would not be poor anymore. However, the Bureau of Labor Statistics reports that 32 percent of our nation's poor people can be classified as "working poor" *(www.census.gov/hhes/poverty/poverty01/table3.pdf)*. The working poor are people who have jobs and still do not earn enough to pay the bills and get ahead. In this session participants will see the connection between their own work experience as an employee and that of the working poor. They will examine wages, learn how much a dollar buys, and discover how much money a family must earn to live above the poverty threshold. Participants also will look at what the Church teaches about just wages and work.

Outcomes

- ◆ The participants will assess their own knowledge of the value of wages.
- ◆ The participants will comprehend some of the economic realities of poverty.
- ◆ The participants will see the plight of low-income workers through the lens of the Scriptures and of Catholic social teaching.
- ◆ The participants will use the knowledge gained to take action on behalf of poor people.

Background Reading

- ◆ Scriptural connections: Jer. 22:13 (Do not cheat workers.), Matt. 20:1–5 (parable concerning wages), 2 Cor. 8:1–16 (encouragement to be generous)
- ◆ *Catholic Youth Bible* article connections: "Dangers of Money" (1 Tim. 6:6–10), "Money Talks" (2 Chron. 9:13–28), "The Greed Trap" (Luke 12:13–28)

Core Session: Exactly What Is a Just Wage? (60 minutes)

Preparation

- Gather the following items:
  - ❑ newsprint
  - ❑ markers
  - ❑ a *Catholic Youth Bible* or other Bible
  - ❑ name tags
- Make double-sided copies of resource 5, "Things We Have," on cardstock, and cut them apart to make a small deck of cards. Make enough copies so that each small group of three to four participants has three sets of cards. See the instructions on the handout for further preparation instructions.
- Choose an action step for the participants to complete from the options listed within the session. The first two options can be done with minimal preparation. The last two options may take more time to prepare and execute. Each option requires unique preparation.

Involve: What We Have (20 minutes)

1. Welcome the participants to the session. Introduce the session by saying:

- Thanks for being here today. How many of you hold part-time jobs?

Ask the participants to respond to this and the following questions by raising their hands.

- How many of you are paid minimum wage for your work?
- How many of you are responsible for your own expenses, such as clothes, entertainment, car (including gas and insurance), school, and so forth?

Now say to the participants:

- Many of you might say there's never enough money to go around for all the things you want.
- Today, our session introduces us to the concept of "just wages." Using real-life statistics, we will look at how much money a family must earn to live above the poverty threshold.
- We will learn what the Catholic Church, through its social teaching, and the Scriptures say about the dignity of workers and why it is important for workers to receive a just wage.
- Finally, we will investigate ways we can take action on behalf of poor people.

2. Ask the participants to organize into groups of four. Distribute to each group three sets of the cards you have created from resource 5, "Things We Have." Present the cards to each group face up. Ask them not to look at the back of the cards until you tell them to do so.

3. Ask the participants to imagine three families in this way:

- All three families have four members.
- The first, family A, lives in luxury. They have all the material things they want, and they are able to buy what they do not have.
- The second, family B, has to watch their spending. They cannot afford everything, so they must make decisions about what they choose to buy, or they could quickly fall into debt.
- The third, family C, lives on the edge of poverty. They have no extras, and every month they wonder whether there will be enough money to pay the bills.

4. Instruct the small groups to review the first set of cards and to decide which items family A would own. Ask the participants to lay out the cards representing those possessions in a row. Allow a few minutes for the groups to complete this task.

5. Tell the groups to use the second and the third set of cards to repeat the process and create separate rows of possessions for family B and for family C. Again, allow a few minutes for the groups to complete this task.

6. Conduct a large group discussion using the following questions:

- What items does family A have? family B?
- What items did you eliminate as the money got tighter?
- What things were you unwilling to take away from family C?

Be sure to allow feedback and comments from each of the small groups, as it is likely that answers may vary.

7. Pose the following question for participants to discuss in their small group:

- How much money do you think each of the families has to earn every year to maintain their style of living?

Ask each small group to report to the large group the amount they think each family must earn. Record the amounts on newsprint. Say to the participants:

- Now that you have discussed in your small groups and made a guess as to what the different families can probably afford, based on your general understanding of their financial situation, let us see how close you are to the real situation.

TryThis

Rather than just reading the information to the participants, consider a visual presentation. Draw on newsprint simple pictures with the money amount. For example, draw four stick figures to represent a family, and put $17,650 next to them. Then draw a house to represent rent, and put the dollar amount for rent next to the figure.

Explore: Presenting Poverty (10 minutes)

1. Include the following information in a short presentation to the participants:

• The Catholic Campaign for Human Development (CCHD) reports the following information about living in the United States in 2002 (for annual updated statistics go to *www.usccb.org/cchd*, and click on "PovertyUSA"):

   ○ The federal poverty threshold for a family of four is $17,650, however, the actual cost of living is much higher. Let's add it up.

   ○ The median annual rent in a major U.S. city is $8,256.

   ○ Annual utility and public service costs total $1,944.

   ○ Bus transportation costs for one year for two people going to and from work, not including trips to the store, doctor, and so forth, average $1,500.

   ○ After government subsidies, a family of four will still spend $1,301 per year on food away from home.

   ○ Even after an employer contribution, a family health plan can cost $1,347 annually.

   ○ Families in poverty with two children under age five will spend $4,200 for child care.

• All of this amounts to a total of $18,548. This amount is almost $1,000 above the poverty threshold, and it includes only the basics.

2. Invite the participants to consider the following question:

• What items does your family C have that were not included in this budget I just presented?

Allow some time for group discussion, and then continue the presentation as follows:

• Although the federal poverty threshold is $17,650, CCHD found that for a two-parent, two-child family, a basic annual family budget ranges from $27,005 a year to $52,114. This varies from one community to another, but the national median is $33,511, approximately twice the poverty threshold.

3. Invite the participants to consider the following questions:

• How much did you estimate that family C would need to earn?

• Was your amount close to these numbers?

4. Allow some time for group discussion, and then continue the presentation with the following illustration.

• Imagine that a single parent heads family C. For that parent to earn more than the federal poverty threshold, he or she must make almost $8.50/hour (40hr/wk × 52wk/yr = 2,080 hours; $17,650 ÷ 2,080 hours = $8.48/hr). This amount is $3.33 above the current minimum wage.

TryThis

Another option for presenting some of the preceding information is to take the tour of PovertyUSA from the Catholic Campaign for Human Development (CCHD) Web site at *www. usccb.org/cchd/povetyusa/index. htm*.

- Even two full-time workers earning minimum wage would earn only $21,424 per year. This is not quite $4,000 above the poverty threshold and far below the national median, yet employers can legally pay these wages to full-time employees with families.

Reflect: The Church on Wages (10 minutes)

1. Begin this segment by presenting the following information:

- The Church has long been in support of the just wage theory. In *Rerum Novarum* (On Capital and Labor), the first document of Catholic social teaching, written in 1891, Pope Leo XIII addresses the issue of just wages.
- Pope Leo XIII writes that a worker's wages should be sufficient to enable him to maintain himself, his wife, and his children in reasonable comfort (*Rerum Novarum,* no. 46).
- Pope Leo XIII also states that two important characteristics are present in labor that make it deserving of a just wage. First, labor is personal; the effort of an individual put forth in labor is solely the possession of the worker. An employer who benefits from such effort should compensate the laborer fairly. Second, labor is also necessary. By no other means can the worker live and provide for a family, so just compensation must be made for work (*Rerum Novarum,* no. 44).
- Later Church documents echo and build upon the idea of just wages introduced in *Rerum Novarum.*
- Nationally, the United States Conference of Catholic Bishops supports raising the minimum wage as one step toward assuring that workers are able to earn enough to support themselves *(www.usccb.org/sdwp/national/ minwageback.htm).*
- The federally determined minimum wage affects workers across the country. Raising the minimum wage can assure that full-time workers earn enough to rise above the poverty threshold.
- In some locations, churches and dioceses support *living wage* campaigns. A living wage ordinance differs from the minimum wage law in that it affects only a small area and often only certain workers. City and county governments are entities likely to enact living wage laws.
- A living wage law sets a minimum amount—determined to be sufficient to support a family—that employers who hold government contracts must pay their workers. In this way, public money used to pay government contracts does not subsidize poverty-level wages. The theory is that workers who earn higher salaries through living wage laws will be better able to support themselves and use fewer public subsidies (such as food stamps or housing assistance) to survive.
- In the case of raising the minimum wage or instituting a living wage, the Church recognizes the dignity of workers. Work allows individuals to

support themselves. Work is also the means by which people contribute to society and make use of the gifts given them by God.

- The dignity of work is recognized in a just wage, for just wages allow people to support themselves and their families without reliance on charity. (*Economic Justice for All,* USCCB, 1984; *A Catholic Framework for Economic Life,* USCCB, 1996; USCCB Office for Social Development and World Peace, *www.usccb.org/sdwp*)

2. Invite a participant to proclaim Matt. 20:1–16. Allow a few moments for quiet reflection. Then ask the participants what they heard being said about wages. Be sure to incorporate these comments into the discussion:

- All the workers were being paid a just wage.
- Scholars think that the one denarius was the amount a laborer would need to earn to support his family for one day.
- In giving each worker this wage, the landowner guaranteed that all the workers, no matter how long they worked, received enough to survive. While this seemingly was not fair to all the workers, it was just.
- We are called to make sure that all workers are treated with this form of justice—that they can earn enough to live in reasonable comfort.

3. Invite the groups to return to the list of items they gave to family C. Ask:

- Are there other things that the family should and would be afforded in a just society?

Discuss their ideas in the large group.

Act: Take Action (10 minutes)

Select one of the following action ideas to use with the participants:

- Prior to the session, visit the Web site of the United States Conference of Catholic Bishops at *www.usccb.org.* Go to the Department of Social Development and World Peace, and find out the latest news on the campaign to raise the minimum wage (select "Domestic Social Development," then click on "Labor Issues" to find "Minimum Wage"). Share the latest updates and background information with the participants. Then invite them to write letters to the senators and representatives indicated in the update, urging the action supported by the USCCB. Provide a template for their letter.
- Review the list of items that family C lives without. In the large group, discuss the implications of living without these things. Ask the participants to pledge to spend the next week abstaining from the use of these items. Schedule a time to report on the experience of going without these items.

- Support your local living wage campaign. Is your city or county considering a living wage ordinance? Find out by talking to your local government leaders, contacting your diocesan social justice office, or visiting *www.livingwagecampaign.org.* Support efforts in your community to enact a living wage, or start your own campaign.
- Find out which workers in your community earn poverty-level wages by talking to your diocesan social justice office, the local Catholic Charities office, or other agencies that work with poor people. Learn more about what you can do to advocate better wages by inviting a guest speaker who works with low-income workers or someone who advocates better wages. Find out what you can do to be an advocate for low-wage earners.

Pray: Prayer for Workers (10 minutes)

Preparation

- Gather the following items:
  - ❑ a cloth
  - ❑ a *Catholic Youth Bible* or other Bible
  - ❑ a pillar candle and matches
  - ❑ items associated with various types of workers, such as a musical instrument, boots, a hammer or other tool, a packet of seeds, furniture polish and a cloth, an apron, or a calculator
- Establish a prayer center in the space you will be using for this session. Cover a small table with a colorful cloth. Arrange a Bible, a candle, and a few items associated with various types of workers, such as a musical instrument, boots, a hammer or other tool, a packet of seeds, furniture polish and cloth, an apron, or a calculator on the table. Put the prayer center where it will be visible during the session, allowing enough space around the table for participants to gather comfortably for prayer.
- Select a gathering song and a closing song with the theme of justice.
- Recruit a reader to proclaim the Scripture passage at Sir. 38:24–34.
- On newsprint, write the response:
  - All who labor maintain the fabric of the world.

   1. Begin the prayer by inviting participants to pause for a moment of silence as they meditate on people who work. Invite them to join with you in singing the opening song you have chosen. Then say:

- Our prayer today asks us to reflect on the workers in the world. Our prayer table has symbols of various workers: farm workers, housekeepers, builders, and musicians. We will listen to the words of Sirach, a teacher who lived in the second century B.C. in Jerusalem, as he speaks about those who work.
- The process for our prayer is listening to the Scriptures, reflecting on a question, and then praying for workers.
- I invite you to be attentive as we now hear the Word of God proclaimed.

Spirit & Song connections

- "Lead Me, Lord," by John D. Becker
- "There Is a Longing," by Anne Quigley
- "We Will Serve the Lord," by Rory Cooney
- "What Is Our Service to Be," by Scot Crandal

Try This

Invite the participants to call out the types of workers they have encountered who work hard and do necessary labor but earn little for their efforts.

Media connections

- *Living Wage Campaigns: An Activist's Guide to Building the Movement for Economic Justice.* This comprehensive 180-page guide for organizing living wage campaigns is designed to help living wage activists get started on a campaign. Substantial portions of this guide are now available at *www.laborstudies.wayne.edu.*

◆ LaborNet provides streaming video on different labor issues from around the world at *www.labornet.net.*

2. Invite the reader to come forward and proclaim Sir. 38:24–26. Allow a few moments for quiet reflection to follow. Then invite the participants to reflect on this question:

• Who are the people who work in the fields, planting, growing, and harvesting the food that sustains us every day?

Pause for a moment of silence. Then say:

• After each prayer, your response will be
  All who labor maintain the fabric of the world.

You may wish to note that you have posted the response on newsprint, where participants may refer to it. Say:

• We pray for those who work.
  All who labor maintain the fabric of the world.

3. Invite the reader to proclaim Sir. 38:27. Allow a few moments for quiet reflection. Then invite the participants to reflect on this question:

• Artists in our culture are often revered and wealthy. They are musicians, actors, designers, but what about those who help keep our communities beautiful? The trash collectors and janitors who care for our public spaces work for much less.

Pause for a moment of silence. Then say:

• We pray for those who work.
  All who labor maintain the fabric of the world.

4. Invite the reader to proclaim Sir. 38:28–30. Allow a few moments for quiet reflection. Then invite the participants to reflect on this question:

• Many people in our communities work hard for little thanks—meat packers, housekeepers, migrant farm workers (insert other professions in your local community). Lift up in prayer the hard workers you know who are not well compensated for their labor.

Pause for a moment of silence. Then say:

• We pray for those who work.
  All who labor maintain the fabric of the world.

5. Invite the reader to come forward and proclaim Sir. 38:31–34. Allow a few moments for quiet reflection. Then say:

• We pray for those who work.
  All who labor maintain the fabric of the world.

6. Invite the participants to pray aloud the Lord's Prayer by saying this or something similar:

• As we remember all those who labor, let us pray together the prayer Jesus taught us.

7. Invite the participants to join in singing the closing song you have chosen.

Things We Have

Copy this resource onto card stock. The COMMENT side is to be copied on the back of the ITEM side. Cut along dotted lines. Each small group needs three sets of cards.

House	Electricity	Video Camera
Apartment	Running Water	Television Game System
Vacation Home	Thrift-shop Clothes	Microwave
Old Car	Plenty of New Clothes	Washing Machine
Used Car	Clothes	Clothes Dryer
Luxury Car	Sports Equipment	Lawn Mower
SUV	Cable Television	Riding Lawn Mower
Second Car	Satellite Television	Boat
Third Car	Phone Service	Jet-Ski
Bicycle	Cell Phone	Daily Paper
Bus Pass	Cell Phone	Magazine
Health Insurance	Cell Phone	Magazine
Comprehensive Car Insurance	Cell Phone	Magazine
Liability-Only Car Insurance	Television	Fast Food
Life Insurance	Television	Dinner Out
Day Care	Television	Movie at a Theater
Babysitter	Television	Piano
Nanny	VCR	Musical Instrument
Private School	VCR	Musical Instrument
College Tuition	DVD Player	Summer Camp
Furniture	Stereo	Summer Camp
Garage Sale Furniture	CD Player	Vacation
Bed	Computer	Vacation
Bed	PDA	Home Swimming Pool
Bed	Internet Access at Home	Swimming Pool Pass
Table and Chairs	Digital Camera	Fitness Club Membership
Refrigerator	Camera	Home Basketball Court
Heat	Film	

	What would you be without if your electricity was disconnected?	
	The state will remove children from a home if water service is disconnected.	
Do you know how to warm up leftovers without a microwave?	How would you feel about yourself if your only clothing was what someone else gave away?	
		The expense of even a used car can be far beyond the means of a limited income.
Children in the central city have less exposure to yards, grass, and parks.		
	Looking for work is difficult without a stable phone number.	
Millions of people read the newspaper daily, a luxury of time and money for many low-wage earners.		
		How hard would it be for you to take public transportation everywhere you went?
		16.5% of the U.S. population lacks health insurance.
		Insurance protects you. If you have none you must do without when something goes wrong.
How often do you stop for a burger or fries without thinking about it? How many people can't?		
How many talented musicians never had access to an instrument?		
		Saving for the future is not always an option.
	How much more difficult would school be without easy access to a home computer?	Where do families sleep if they don't have enough beds?
	Families with no camera or film often have few pictures of their children as keepsakes.	Eating is expensive with no place to store cold food. Refrigerators are expensive and hard to move.

6 Working for the Common Good

Overview

With so many needs in the world, it is understandable that people occasionally assume there is nothing meaningful they can do to help. Assuming there is too little to go around of whatever is needed, they hide or hoard what they have for their personal and family use. Our Catholic faith offers a startlingly different perspective. Rather than starting with a mentality of scarcity (too many needs and too little to share), faith offers an image of abundance—a deep-seated belief that God has provided more than enough to meet everyone's needs. Faith tells us that everyone benefits when we believe in God's providence, look to the common good, and share what we have. This session explores the theme of the common good as a basic tenet of Catholic social teaching and brings participants to an awareness of the power they have to bring about positive change in the world.

Outcomes

- The participants will explore the often-difficult balance between meeting their personal needs and contributing to the benefit of others.
- The participants will uphold the values of common good and stewardship and incorporate them in their personal decision-making process.
- The participants will examine their personal time, talent, and treasure and make decisions about how they can use these God-given gifts to promote both the personal and the common good.

Background Reading

- Scriptural connections: Heb. 13:16 (what is pleasing to God), Matt. 25:14–30 (parable of the talents), Luke 3:11 (Share what we have.)
- *Catholic Youth Bible* article connections: "Christians Share Their Money out of Solidarity" (2 Cor., chaps. 8–9), "Stewardship" (Acts 4:32–37), "Stewardship: Making a Contribution" (Luke 21:1–4)

Core Session: Working for the Common Good (70 minutes)

- Involve: Stone Soup (10 minutes)
- Explore: Unpacking the Story (5 minutes)
- Reflect: Adding Your Piece to the Pot (15 minutes)
- Reflect: A Jubilee Feast (10 minutes)
- Act: A Commitment to the Common Good (10 minutes)
- Pray: Living Jubilee (20 minutes)

Core Session: Working for the Common Good (70 minutes)

Preparation

- Gather the following items:
  - ❑ *Catholic Youth Bibles* or other Bibles, one for each participant
  - ❑ newsprint
  - ❑ markers
  - ❑ sheets of blank paper or index cards, one for each participant
  - ❑ pens or pencils
  - ❑ copies of handout 5, "A Jubilee Prayer," one for each participant
- Read the "Stone Soup" story found in step 1 of this session and be prepared to tell the tale in your own words.
- Recruit a reader to proclaim John 6:1–14.

Involve: Stone Soup (10 minutes)

1. Welcome the participants, and provide an overview of the session. Then say:

- I am going to tell you a story called "Stone Soup," which comes, like soup, in many versions. Listen to the story, and think about variations of the story you may have heard. Reflect on what the story tells you about human nature and about people's willingness to share.
- On their way home from war, three soldiers drew near to a small country village. They were tired and hungry from their travel and wanted nothing more than a simple meal and a place to rest their weary bodies.
- The villagers, spotting the soldiers in the distance and fearful they would be asked for or robbed of what they had, concealed their food and valuables. They quickly hid in their homes, awaiting a sudden knock on the door and a demand for help.
- The expected knock came, and the soldiers' request for help (more polite and much less demanding than expected) was universally denied. Having made the rounds of all the village homes with nothing to show for their effort, the soldiers put their heads together and decided on a new approach to fill their empty bellies.
- Calling the villagers together, the soldiers announced that they, hungry as they were, also sensed the villagers' hunger pangs. Amazingly, they offered to prepare a special meal for everyone in the village made from just three round stones! The largest pot in the village was quickly filled with water and set to boil. The soldiers carefully selected and added to the pot three round stones from the side of the road.

- As the water started to bubble, one soldier commented that as good as the feast would be, the soup would probably taste better with just a bit of salt and pepper. One of the villagers dashed into her house and returned with the requested spices, adding them to the brew.
- Noting how poor the village was, a second soldier lamented the absence of a carrot or two to add to the stew—a small item, but one that would complement the stones so well. A bunch of carrots, drawn from their hiding place in a villager's loft, was quickly added. Then, slowly, beef bones . . . and potatoes . . . and cabbage . . . and barley . . . and cream . . . made their way into the pot.
- As the pleasant smell filled the air, mouths began to water—and the villagers realized how much better the soup would be with a bit of bread . . . and butter . . . and a mug of cider . . . and a piece of cake or fruit for dessert. The foodstuffs were gathered, tables were arranged in the village square, and all ate to their heart's content. With their stomachs full, the soldiers were shown to comfortable beds for the night.
- The next morning, the soldiers packed the magic stones in their knapsacks, said goodbye to their newfound friends, and left everyone in the village amazed at the feast prepared with just three round stones!

(This summary draws on several versions of the Stone Soup tale, most notably that authored by Marcia Brown and first published in 1947. To read the story in full, check out *Marcia Brown, Stone Soup: An Old Tale Retold* [New York: Aladdin Books, 1986].)

Explore: Unpacking the Story (5 minutes)

1. Invite the participants to share reactions to the story. Ask them to share the moral of the story and what the story reveals about human nature, sharing, or solutions to hunger.

Reflect: Adding Your Piece to the Pot (15 minutes)

1. Share the following comments as a transition from the stories of childhood to the stories of faith:

- Stone Soup is a simple but powerful story. Apart from the humor the story brings forth, it is valuable because of the truths it reveals. Two of these truths are mirrored in our Catholic justice tradition and Church teaching on *stewardship* and the *common good*.
- The concept of *stewardship* reminds us that all we are and everything we have are gifts from God. God has created the world in such a way that there is enough of everything for everyone . . . if we only learn to share it properly.

TryThis

- Instead of retelling the version above, visit the children's section of your local library or bookstore, and pick out an illustrated version to share. Conduct a "show and tell" with the group, reading the story and sharing the illustrations.
- Use props—a big pot, three large stones, salt and pepper, carrots, and other ingredients to use as illustrations when you tell the story.
- Work with several participants prior to the session to perform a dramatic reading or presentation of the story, using different voices for each character.

TryThis

After retelling the original story, ask small groups to create a new version, updated with modern characters, setting, and language. If time allows, illustrate this new version, and perhaps share it with local groups of children.

- In place of a mentality of scarcity (a belief that there isn't enough of every-thing to go around and that the wise person hides or hoards what he or she has for the sake of self, family, and friends), *stewardship* offers an image of abundance (a belief that God, in his providence, provides everything we need in ample quantity) and promotes sharing as a natural way of life.
- God's gifts to us are many and varied—food and drink, health and edu-cation, talent and ability, companionship and love, faith and wonder. God has been generous in sharing these gifts with us and asks us to be equally generous in sharing these same gifts with others.
- *Stewardship,* then, is about the way we care for ourselves, for one another, and for our world.
- *Common good,* for its part, is about how we see ourselves in relationship to those around us. Do we view our need for others as a blessing or a curse? Are we driven more by competition or by cooperation? Are we out strictly for our own good, or do the needs and wants of others come into play in our life choices and decisions?
- *Common good* proclaims that we are linked to one another and that our decisions need to be made in a way that benefits all.

2. Invite participants to join you in a conversation about stewardship and the common good. Use questions like the following to prompt discus-sion and dialogue:
- How do you see the values of stewardship and concern for the common good promoted in the world today?
- Where do you see these values pushed aside or openly rejected?
- What makes these principles valuable and attractive as a way of life?
- What makes living them out difficult and challenging?
- Offer examples of how sharing one's talents and working for the common good can benefit both the individual and the group as a whole.

The participants can draw examples from their family, school, or work expe-rience—or relate it to what they see in the world at large.

Reflect: A Jubilee Feast (10 minutes)

1. Invite the reader to come forward and proclaim John 6:1–14. Allow a few moments for quiet reflection. Then say:
- In addition to John's account, the story is told, with variations, by Matthew, Mark, and Luke. Obviously, it is a story that spoke loudly to the people of Jesus' day, and it remains equally powerful for us today.
- This story and similar ones drawn from both the Old and the New Testaments, speak eloquently of God's concern for the hungry and God's ability to turn nature upside down occasionally to accomplish what God wants.

TryThis

As an alternative to the large group discussion, invite the participants to organize into small groups. Ask each group to concentrate on one of the following settings: family, school, church, local commu-nity, or government programs and policies. After ample time for discussion, invite a representative from each small group to share its example with the larger group.

- The story of Jesus' multiplication of the loaves and fishes has been expanded on by several storytellers. Although these stories are not "gospel truth," they can help us look at Jesus' miracles in a new and exciting way.
- One version tells the story straight through but suggests that it was not the *law of nature* that Jesus turned on its head to feed the 5,000. It was, instead, *human nature* that Jesus transformed—people's tendency to hide their limited food when there wasn't a restaurant in sight or much likelihood that they would have anything to eat on the long journey home. The author of this story wonders which would be the greater miracle: providing supper for 5,000 from just a small basket of fish and bread or opening the hearts of 5,000 to spontaneous sharing—joyfully setting their own hunger aside to feed the countless others around them (Albert Nolan, *Jesus Before Christianity* [Maryknoll, NY: Orbis Books, 2001]).

2. Ask the participants to respond to the following question:
- Which do you think would be the greater miracle? Why?

After hearing their comments, summarize by stating that the story provides a clear lesson on the demands of stewardship and the common good.

3. To bring this segment to a close, note that the Old Testament, like the New Testament, has much to teach us about stewardship and the common good. Suggest that although there is not time in the session to take a close look at Old Testament thought on these issues, it would be a mistake to leave the Scriptures without at least mentioning the concept of jubilee year. Include the following points in your presentation:

- The people of the Old Testament realized that it was sometimes difficult to maintain control over their lives. People lost their jobs or got sick. Crops were ruined by flood or lack of rain. Individuals made poor financial decisions or, through no fault of their own, ran into a string of bad luck. Whatever the reason, the result was the same—they lost control over their lives and found it difficult to climb back to self-sufficiency.
- Accordingly, every fiftieth year was declard a jubilee year, a chance for the poor and needy to start over with all the basics needed for survival: personal freedom, a place of their own, the necessary possessions, and no major debts.
- Jubilee takes the concepts of stewardship and common good and plays them out, not just on the personal level, but also on the level of society at large. Stewardship and decision making based on an understanding of the common good are concepts intended not just for individuals but also for society as a whole!

Act: A Commitment to the Common Good (10 minutes)

1. Distribute a blank sheet of paper or an index card and a pen or pencil to the participants. Note that hunger and need were very real problems in Jesus' time and that, unfortunately, they remain equally problematic today. Suggest that hunger and all the big issues facing our world today would benefit from a faith response that takes stewardship and concern for the common good seriously. Ask participants:

- What is a problem facing the world today—locally or globally?
- How can a Christian approach to stewardship and the common good turn the problem around?

Invite the participants to take a moment to reflect on and write down a problem or concern they see in the world and how a commitment to stewardship and the common good would make a difference.

2. Then invite a few participants to share their responses out loud. Record their responses on newsprint.

3. Suggest that—like the young person in John's Gospel who offered a small basket of fish and bread to Jesus—they too can be part of the solution to the problems they have named. Make the following comments:

- Keep your eyes and ears attuned in the coming week to the need and hardship experienced by others.
- When you hear about problems, stop for a moment and reflect on how you can use your available time, abundant talent and abilities, limited funds, and access to other resources (education, transportation, and so forth) to help ease people's suffering and lessen the problem's hold on the world.

Pray: Living Jubilee (20 minutes)

Preparation

- Gather the following items:
  - ❑ construction paper
  - ❑ scissors
  - ❑ pens
  - ❑ an audiocassette or CD player
  - ❑ audiocassettes or CDs of reflective instrumental music
  - ❑ a picnic-style tablecloth
  - ❑ a *Catholic Youth Bible* or other Bible
  - ❑ a cross
  - ❑ a pillar candle and matches
  - ❑ a small picnic basket
  - ❑ a few napkins
  - ❑ seasonal decorations

Spirit & Song
connections

- ◆ "Find Us Ready," by Tom Booth
- ◆ "Song of the Body of Christ," adapted by David Haas

- Using colored construction paper, create silhouettes of fish and loaves of bread. You will need five images for each participant.
- Choose a gathering song and a closing song with the theme of stewardship and/or giving.
- Establish a prayer center in the space you will be using for this session. Lay a picnic-style tablecloth on a table (or on the floor). Arrange a Bible, a cross, a candle, a small picnic basket, a few napkins, and any seasonal decoration you deem appropriate on the table. Put the prayer center where it will be visible during the session, allowing enough space around the table for participants to gather comfortably for prayer.
- Before beginning the prayer service, distribute a pen, five fish or loaf of bread cutouts, and a copy of handout 5, "A Jubilee Prayer," to each participant.

1. Invite the participants to gather around the prayer table. Ask them to join in singing the gathering song you have chosen.

2. Drawing the participants' attention to the fish and loaf of bread cutouts, say:
- Reflect quietly on the gifts you can bring to Jesus—not the literal loaves and fishes, but your personal treasures such as available time, abundant talent and abilities, limited funds, access to education, transportation, and so forth.
- Write the name of a gift on one side of a fish or bread silhouette. On the other side, write a brief description of how your gift can be used for the common good. Helping to feed people's hunger for food, shelter, freedom, and companionship are a few examples.

Allow several minutes for the young people to complete this reflection. You may wish to play instrumental music in the background during this time.

3. Invite the participants to come forward quietly and prayerfully, one at a time, and place their gifts in the picnic basket. As they do so, invite them to share one gift and how it can be used for the common good. Those who prefer not to share can place their gifts in the basket.

4. Then say to the participants:
- We have heard many challenges during this session, and we know Jesus is with us as we try to meet these challenges in our everyday lives. As a sign of our commitment to work for the common good, let us recite the Jubilee Prayer together.

Refer the participants to handout 5, and begin the prayer as noted. At the close of prayer, encourage participants to take the Jubilee Prayer home and recite it daily during the coming week.

A Jubilee Prayer

Loving God, we are the work of your hands.
Life and all the good things of our world are gifts from you.

We thank you for the many ways you have blessed us and our land.
Help us to remember your goodness and to accept the challenge of
    sharing who we are and what we have with others.

Help us to freely share our time and talent with others.

Give us the confidence we need to speak out for those whose needs
    remain unmet.

Help us to be as generous in sharing our possessions and resources with
    others as you have been in sharing your gifts of life and love with us.
We ask this in the name of Jesus, our teacher and our friend, now and forever.

Amen.

(This prayer is from "The Story of Faith," in *FaithWays,* by the Center for Ministry Development
[Naugatuck, CT: Center for Ministry Development, 1996], page 91. Copyright © 1996 by the
Center for Ministry Development. Used with permission.)

7

Caring for Creation:
Environmental Justice

Overview

Whether we live in a big city, a rural area, a small town, or the suburbs, we affect our environment. The actions of people cause changes to the world around us. Some of these changes can stress and damage the earth's natural systems. In this session participants examine the environment, explore the dangers that threaten the environment locally, nationally, and internationally, and reflect on an environmental statement from the U.S. Catholic bishops. Participants will also choose a personal or group strategy for doing their part to renew the earth.

Outcomes

◆ The participants will gain a greater appreciation for the environment.
◆ The participants will realize the scope of environmental challenges in the world.
◆ The participants will understand Church teaching about caring for the environment by studying the Scripture, Catholic social teachings and the *Catechism.*
◆ The participants will have the opportunity to explore action strategies for doing their part to renew the earth.

Background Reading

◆ Scriptural connections: Gen. 1:1–31 (six days of creation), Gen. 2:15 (another account of creation), Job 38: 4–30 (The Lord answers Job.)

**Core Session:
Caring for Creation:
Environmental Justice
(80 minutes)**

◆ Involve: Experiencing the Environment
(10 minutes)
◆ Involve: Imagine This
(10 minutes)
◆ Explore: In the News
(20 minutes)
◆ Reflect: Renewing the Earth
(15 minutes)
◆ Act: Action Ideas
(5 minutes)
◆ Pray: Praying with Saint Francis of Assisi
(20 minutes)

Core Session: Caring for Creation: Environmental Justice (80 minutes)

Preparation

- Gather the following items:
  - ❑ pens or pencils
  - ❑ sheets of blank paper, one for each participant
  - ❑ scissors, one or two for each small group
  - ❑ newspapers featuring local, national, and world news and/or news magazines such as *Time* or *Newsweek,* several for each small group
  - ❑ newsprint
  - ❑ markers
  - ❑ masking tape
  - ❑ copies of handout 7, "Action Ideas," one for each participant
- Copy resource 6, "Renewing the Earth Quotes." Cut the quotes apart so each small group can work with two or three quotes (there are 12 in all).
- Decide which of the suggested quotes will be given as reading assignments.

Involve: Experiencing the Environment (10 minutes)

1. Welcome the participants, and provide an overview of the session. Give each participant a pen or pencil and a sheet of paper. Then invite the participants to walk outside with you. Once everyone is outside, provide these instructions:

- Make a list of all the things you see in your immediate surroundings that are a part of the environment. Include items that are natural and those items that are made by people.

Allow about 5 minutes for participants to complete their task. When finished, return to the meeting space.

2. On a sheet of newsprint, create two headings:

- Created by God
- Made by People

Ask the participants, one at a time, to name items from their list and indicate under which heading the item should appear. Examples of items created by God might include trees, earth, clouds, birds, people, and so forth. Examples of items made by people might include buildings, cars, signs, pavement, trash, and so forth. Continue until all the participants' items are listed on the newsprint.

Imagine This (10 minutes)

1. Ask the participants to imagine this far-fetched situation:

Try This

If going outdoors is not possible, ask the participants to answer the question:

◆ "If you could spend one day anywhere in the world, where would you go?"

Give sample destinations such as the Rocky Mountains, Disney World, Miami Beach, Paris, Yellowstone, and so forth. When participants have decided where to spend the day, have them create a list of the things they would see in the place they chose. Continue with the activity as directed above.

- Space aliens have arrived on earth. It is obvious that they are technologically superior to us. While earthlings everywhere are frightened of what the aliens might do, initial calls to use force to send the aliens on their way are quickly dismissed as foolish.
- However, it is not long before the aliens send a representative to speak to a gathering of world leaders. The alien representative tells the world leaders that this will be the aliens' only stop on our planet, and the mother ship requires only one thing from the blue planet: all our cars and spare auto parts (or buildings, or some other significant item listed on the "Made by People" list). Instantly, every car and car part on the planet disappears. There are no more cars anywhere. The alien representative says, "Thank you!" and disappears.
- What would happen on earth as a result of this scenario?

Record the participants' answers on newsprint. Participants are likely to make suggestions such as: We would walk more. I would have to ride my bike to school. Subways and buses would be more crowded. Someone may even say, "We would make more cars." If this point isn't raised after a reasonable amount of time, make the suggestion yourself.

2. Say to the participants:
- It is inevitable in this scenario that humans would make more cars, and although it would take considerable time, almost everyone would eventually have a replacement car.
- Now imagine a slightly different situation. Humanity encounters the same aliens, the same representative with the same desire for only one thing on earth, but in this story it is not cars and car parts the aliens want. This time the aliens want all our trees. They want living trees, felled trees, leaves, seeds, acorns, pine cones, and so forth. In the next instant, all the trees on earth are gone.
- What would happen on earth as a result of this scenario?

Continue the discussion as the participants come to realize that unlike with cars, we cannot just make more trees to replace the ones that were taken.

3. Share with the participants the following thoughts:
- We know how to make cars; we do not know how to make trees.
- God created nature. People make things. Although humanity has made great advances in manipulating the natural world to do some incredible things, we still cannot replicate God's creative ability.
- We can continue to reproduce people. We can breed animals and cultivate plants, but once a species or a resource is gone, it is gone forever.
- As we continue to use the earth's resources, create pollution, and increase the population of the planet, we must keep in mind that our environment is fragile and that the products of our environment were given to us by God to be cared for and shared by all.

Mediaconnections

◆ View the video *The Earth is the Lord's* (USCCB Office of Publishing, No. 058-3, 13 minutes). The video presents the Church's view on environmental issues. It can be ordered by calling 800-235-8722 or by going to *www.usccb.org.*

Mediaconnections

◆ The Columban Mission Education Office produces the video *Voices of the Earth,* which tells the story of environmental issues in the Philippines. A leadership manual for conducting one group session is included. It is available on a free loan program by calling 402-291-1920 or ordering online at *www.columban. org/missioned.*

TryThis

◆ If you have access to the Internet, allow one or more groups to search news sites for recent articles about environmental issues instead of using newspapers and magazines.

◆ Instead of having the participants research environmental issues in a newspaper or magazine, order copies of the *Youth Update* entitled *Protecting God's Creation*—Y0799 (available from St. Anthony Messenger Press, 800-488-0488 or *www. americancatholic.org*).

Mediaconnections

◆ A great Web site with tips for building and maintaining a composting area is *www.mastercomposter.com*.

TryThis

◆ The USCCB has published *Peace with God the Creator, Peace with All Creation*. The kit includes articles, activities, homily aides, and a prayer card for parishes and parish groups. It is available from the USCCB at 800-235-8722 or *www.usccb.org*.

◆ The National Federation for Catholic Youth Ministry, Inc., has published *Protecting God's Creation*

Explore: In the News (20 minutes)

1. Organize the participants into groups of three to five. Distribute several newspapers and news magazines, as well as one or two scissors to each group. Give these instructions:

• Find and cut out articles that discuss environmental issues on the local, national, or international levels. Look for articles that address recycling programs, local development (such as new housing and shopping centers), urban sprawl, fuel efficiency, emission standards, water supply, water or air quality, pollution, land protection, Super Fund sites, animal populations, oil spills, famine, drought, global warming, mining and drilling, energy, agriculture, and so forth.

Allow 5 to 7 minutes for the groups to complete this task. While groups are working on their task, prepare five sheets of newsprint with the following headings: Land, Air, Water, People, and Animals.

2. Invite a representative from each group to briefly report on what they found. As the representatives finish, ask them to tape the articles to the sheet of newsprint where each issue best fits. If some issues fit in more than one category, let the participants decide where to place the article. When the reports are complete, make these comments:

• A great variety of environmental issues faces us today.
• The scope and severity of environmental problems, combined with the lack of agreement on the manner and speed with which issues need to be addressed, can seem overwhelming. Are these environmental problems too large for individuals to address? Why?

Invite some response from the participants. Then continue by saying:

• As people of hope and as members of a faith community, we are named as stewards of God's creation and must do our part to care for nature.

Reflect: Renewing the Earth (15 minutes)

1. Introduce this activity by saying:

• In 1991 the United States Conference of Catholic Bishops released *Renewing the Earth: An Invitation to Reflection and Action on Environment in Light of Catholic Social Teaching*. This short but powerful document raises environmental issues, highlights our Catholic responsibility, and urges action on behalf of the faithful and people of goodwill. We are going to look at a few key statements.

2. Using resource 6, "Renewing the Earth Quotes," provide each group with two to three quotes. You might note that all these quotes are taken directly from the document you just mentioned. Tell the groups they have 10 minutes to:

• read the quotes
• choose the one quote that challenges them the most

- identify the principle or value in the quote
- discuss how the principle is abused or defended in our society
- name three things teenagers can do to live out the principle in their everyday lives

They will be asked to share these last three items with the large group at the end of the discussion.

Act: Action Ideas (15 minutes)

1. Distribute copies of handout 7, "Action Ideas," to the participants. Invite them to read the handout and to choose one action that they are interested in pursuing. Ask participants to form small groups with others who have chosen the same action. Then invite each group to form a plan of action for the next month. A question they may wish to consider is:

- What are you going to do in the next thirty days to care for God's creation?

Ask each group to identify one long-term action they can take (over the next five years) to continue to care for the earth.

2. Invite a spokesperson from each group to share the highlights of the plan with the large group.

Pray: Praying with Saint Francis of Assisi (20 minutes)

Preparation

- Gather the following items:
  - ❑ copies of handout 6, "Canticle of the Sun," one for each participant
  - ❑ small clay (or plastic) 3-inch pots, one for each participant
  - ❑ potting soil, enough to fill the clay pots
  - ❑ vegetable or flower seed packets, enough for a few seeds for each participant
  - ❑ a cloth
  - ❑ a *Catholic Youth Bible* or other Bible
  - ❑ a cross
  - ❑ a pillar candle and matches
  - ❑ an audiocassette or CD player
  - ❑ audiocassettes or CDs of reflective instrumental music
- Select a gathering song and a closing song with the theme of creation.
- Recruit a reader to proclaim Phil. 4:8–9.
- Establish a prayer center in the space you will be using for this session. Cover a small table with a colorful cloth. Arrange a Bible, a cross, and a candle on the table. Put the prayer center where it will be visible during the session, allowing enough space around the table for participants to gather comfortably for prayer. You will need to set the clay pots, potting soil, and seeds near the prayer table.

for use with adolescents. This is a binder resource with six fully developed sessions to help young people explore environmental justice issues. To order, call NFCYM at 202-636-3825, or go to *www.nfcym.org*.

Spirit & Song connections

- ◆ "Let All the Earth," by Steve Angrisano and Tom Tomaszek
- ◆ "Taste and See," by Bob Hurd

Familyconnections

- ◆ Encourage families to conduct a home inspection. Pinpointing things they can change to make their homes more environmentally friendly (use recycled paper products, install low-flow toilets, use phosphate-free detergent, add houseplants, install a solar water heater). Suggest that they determine priorities, schedule improvements, and list responsibilities (adapted from Leif Kehrwald and John Roberto, editors, *Families and Youth: A Resource Manual,* p. 237).

1. Invite the participants to gather around the prayer table. Distribute a copy of handout 6, "Canticle of the Sun," to each participant. Introduce the closing prayer by saying:

- We talked today about the environment, the creation God has entrusted to us. As stewards of this great gift, we are called to be aware of and sensitive to the ways the earth can be threatened.
- We saw evidence of concern about the environment through the news articles and magazine stories. We came up with ideas of how we can help keep our environment healthy.
- Our prayer today helps us connect these stories and images to our faith and gives us hope for a renewed commitment to the care of God's creation.

2. Invite the participants to join in singing the gathering song you have chosen.

3. Ask the reader to come forward and proclaim Phil. 4:8–9. Allow a few moments for quiet reflection. Then say:

- In this reading, we hear Saint Paul encouraging the Philippians to concentrate on those things worthy of praise. Certainly this includes the beauty and wonder of nature. We know that Saint Francis of Assisi had a special affinity for nature.
- As our response to this reading, I invite you to pray the Canticle of the Sun together.

Refer the participants to the handout you have provided, and continue as noted.

4. Invite the participants to approach the prayer table two at a time and select a clay pot, fill it with potting soil, and plant a few seeds. You may wish to play some instrumental music in the background while they complete this task.

5. When they are finished, ask the participants to raise their clay pots as you offer this prayer:

- O God of all that is great and good, bless these small pots and the mystery of life they contain. Encourage us in our efforts to protect and safeguard all of creation as we grow and nurture these plants. Help us to be steadfast stewards of your creation. We pray this in your Son's name. Amen.

6. Conclude by inviting the participants to join in singing the closing song you have selected.

Canticle of the Sun

Praised be you, my Lord, with all your creatures,

especially Sir Brother Sun,

Who is the day and through whom You give us light.

And he is beautiful and radiant with great splendor

And bears a likeness of you, Most High One.

Praised be You, my Lord, through Sister Moon and the stars,

In heaven You formed them clear and precious and beautiful.

Praised be You, my Lord, through Brother Wind

and through the air, cloudy and serene, and every kind of weather

through which You give sustenance to Your creatures.

Praised be You, my Lord, through Sister Water,

which is very useful and humble and precious and chaste.

Praised be You, my Lord, through Brother Fire,

through whom you light the night,

and he is beautiful and playful and robust and strong.

Praised be You, my Lord, through our sister Mother Earth,

who sustains us and governs us,

and who produces varied fruits with colored flowers and herbs.

Praise and bless my Lord and give Him thanks and serve Him with great humility.

Action Ideas

Reduce consumption. We in the United States use more than our share of the world's resources. Curbing our consumption is an important step to aiding the environment. Online sources for future reference include: Ad Busters *(www.adbusters.org)*, Catholic Relief Services *(www.catholicrelief.org)*, Catholic Campaign for Human Development *(www.usccb.org/cchd)*, and Global Issues *(www.globalissues.org)*.

- Turn off lights and appliances and electronics you are not using.
- Do not run water unnecessarily.
- Turn down the heat. Wear an extra layer of clothing to keep warm.
- Carpool, ride a bike, use public transportation.
- Print on both sides of the paper.
- Use compact fluorescent light bulbs.
- Select the "power saver" option in your computer.
- Turn off your computer monitor when it is not being used.
- Drive a fuel-efficient car.
- Limit your use of lawnmowers and snowmobiles. These vehicles emit large amounts of pollution for their size.

Reuse items. We live in a "throw-away" society. Disposable products are often convenient, but the environmental impact is damaging.

- Return your paper and plastic bags to the store, and reuse them.
- Bring your own glass, cup, or mug to meetings and events rather than using disposable products.
- Donate your old clothes to a thrift store or social service agency.
- Start a compost pile.
- Do not litter.
- Do not use commercial fertilizer on your lawn.
- Support the use of renewable products.
- Plant a tree.

Recycle. Recycling products takes a little extra time, but doing so is taking a step toward achieving sustainable consumption.

- Take advantage of the curbside recycling program in your town, or take your recyclables to a local collection site.
- Purchase products made from recycled materials.
- Sponsor an aluminum can or newspaper drive at your church or school.
- Use recycling as a fund-raising opportunity, or donate the money raised to an environmental protection project.
- Make your church or school a recycling collection site. Check with your area recycling service about hosting a collection container, or visit *www.paperretriever.com.*
- Buy used items rather than new ones.

Advocacy. Advocating policies to protect creation or to change the structures and systems that cause damage to the environment is a proactive and powerful action step.

- Support the protection of wild spaces and endangered or threatened animals by learning more and writing letters to your elected officials.
- Shop "green." Visit *www.responsibleshopper.org* for a list of retailers that are environmentally friendly.
- Make a donation online. Support the rain forest by visiting *www.the rainforestsite.org* and make a donation to protect land in the rainforest. Support other environmental projects by visiting *www.earthshare.org.*
- Learn more from organizations that support the environment. Visit *www. gristmagazine.com, www.greenpeace.org,* the Environmental Protection Agency at *www.epa.gov,* or *www.earthday.net.*
- Celebrate Earth Day on April 22 by taking part in community activities.

Renewing the Earth Quotes

After duplicating this resource, cut apart these quotations for use by the small groups.

✂

"At its core, the environmental crisis is a moral challenge. It calls us to examine how we use and share the goods of the earth, what we pass on to future generations, and how we live in harmony with God's creation."

(*Renewing the Earth,* by the United States Conference of Catholic Bishops, from *Pastoral Letters and Statements of the United States Catholic Bishops, Volume VI 1989–1997,* by the United States Conference of Catholic Bishops (USCCB) [Washington DC: USCCB, Inc., 1998], page 397. Copyright © 1998 by the USCCB, Inc.)

"The environmental crisis of our day constitutes an exceptional call to conversion. As individuals, as institutions, as a people, we need a change of heart to save the planet for our children and generations yet unborn."

(*Renewing the Earth,* by the United States Conference of Catholic Bishops, from *Pastoral Letters and Statements of the United States Catholic Bishops, Volume VI 1989–1997,* by the United States Conference of Catholic Bishops (USCCB) [Washington DC: USCCB, Inc., 1998], page 417. Copyright © 1998 by the USCCB, Inc.)

"The human family is charged with preserving the beauty, diversity, and integrity of nature, as well as with fostering its productivity. Yet, God alone is sovereign over the whole earth."

(*Renewing the Earth,* by the United States Conference of Catholic Bishops, from *Pastoral Letters and Statements of the United States Catholic Bishops, Volume VI 1989–1997,* by the United States Conference of Catholic Bishops (USCCB) [Washington DC: USCCB, Inc., 1998], page 402. Copyright © 1998 by the USCCB, Inc.)

"To ensure the survival of a healthy planet, then, we must not only establish a sustainable economy but must also labor for justice both within and among nations. We must seek a society where economic life and environmental commitment work together to protect and to enhance life on this planet."

(*Renewing the Earth,* by the United States Conference of Catholic Bishops, from *Pastoral Letters and Statements of the United States Catholic Bishops, Volume VI 1989–1997,* by the United States Conference of Catholic Bishops (USCCB) [Washington DC: USCCB, Inc., 1998], page 398. Copyright © 1998 by the USCCB, Inc.)

"Our tradition calls us to protect the life and dignity of the human person, and it is increasingly clear that this task cannot be separated from the care and defense of all creation."

(*Renewing the Earth,* by the United States Conference of Catholic Bishops, from *Pastoral Letters and Statements of the United States Catholic Bishops, Volume VI 1989–1997,* by the United States Conference of Catholic Bishops (USCCB) [Washington DC: USCCB, Inc., 1998], page 398. Copyright © 1998 by the USCCB, Inc.)

"The option for the poor embedded in the Gospel and the Church's teaching make us aware that the poor suffer most directly from environmental decline and have the least access to relief from their suffering."

(*Renewing the Earth,* by the United States Conference of Catholic Bishops, from *Pastoral Letters and Statements of the United States Catholic Bishops, Volume VI 1989–1997,* by the United States Conference of Catholic Bishops (USCCB) [Washington DC: USCCB, Inc., 1998], page 408. Copyright © 1998 by the USCCB, Inc.)

"But in most countries today, including our own, it is the poor and the powerless who most directly bear the burden of current environmental carelessness . . . Too often, the structure of sacrifice involved in environmental remedies seems to exact a high price from the poor and from workers . . . [they] shoulder much of the weight of economic adjustment."

(*Renewing the Earth,* by the United States Conference of Catholic Bishops, from *Pastoral Letters and Statements of the United States Catholic Bishops, Volume VI 1989–1997,* by the United States Conference of Catholic Bishops (USCCB) [Washington DC: USCCB, Inc., 1998], page 399. Copyright © 1998 by the USCCB, Inc.)

"Regrettably, advantaged groups often seem more intent on curbing Third World births than on restraining the even more voracious consumerism of the developed world. We believe this compounds injustice and increase disrespect for the life of the weakest among us."

(*Renewing the Earth,* by the United States Conference of Catholic Bishops, from *Pastoral Letters and Statements of the United States Catholic Bishops, Volume VI 1989–1997,* by the United States Conference of Catholic Bishops (USCCB) [Washington DC: USCCB, Inc., 1998], page 409. Copyright © 1998 by the USCCB, Inc.)

"We in the developed world . . . are obligated to address our own wasteful and destructive use of resources as a matter of top priority."

(*Renewing the Earth*, by the United States Conference of Catholic Bishops, from *Pastoral Letters and Statements of the United States Catholic Bishops, Volume VI 1989–1997*, by the United States Conference of Catholic Bishops (USCCB) [Washington DC: USCCB, Inc., 1998], pages 409–410. Copyright © 1998 by the USCCB, Inc.)

"Humanity is at a crossroads. Having read the signs of the times, we can either ignore the harm we see and witness further damage, or we can take up our responsibilities to the Creator and creation with renewed courage and commitment."

(*Renewing the Earth*, by the United States Conference of Catholic Bishops, from *Pastoral Letters and Statements of the United States Catholic Bishops, Volume VI 1989–1997*, by the United States Conference of Catholic Bishops (USCCB) [Washington DC: USCCB, Inc., 1998], page 414. Copyright © 1998 by the USCCB, Inc.)

"We are charged with restoring the integrity of all creation. We must care for all God's creatures, especially the most vulnerable. How, then, can we protect endangered species and at the same time be callous to the unborn, the elderly, or disabled persons? Is not abortion also a sin against creation? If we turn our backs on our own unborn children, can we truly expect that nature will receive respectful treatment at our hands? The care of the earth will not be advanced by the destruction of human life at any stage of development."

(*Renewing the Earth*, by the United States Conference of Catholic Bishops, from *Pastoral Letters and Statements of the United States Catholic Bishops, Volume VI 1989–1997*, by the United States Conference of Catholic Bishops (USCCB) [Washington DC: USCCB, Inc., 1998], pages 410–411. Copyright © 1998 by the USCCB, Inc.)

"A just and sustainable society and world are not an optional ideal, but a moral and practical necessity. Without justice, a sustainable economy will be beyond reach. Without an ecologically responsible world economy, justice will be unachievable. To accomplish either is an enormous task; together they seem overwhelming. But 'all things are possible' to those who hope in God (Mark 10:27). Hope is the virtue at the heart of a Christian environmental ethic, . . . We can proceed with hope because, as at the dawn of creation, so today the Holy Spirit breathes new life into all earth's creatures. Today, we pray with new conviction and concern for all God's creation: Send forth thy Spirit, Lord and renew the face of the earth."

(*Renewing the Earth*, by the United States Conference of Catholic Bishops, from *Pastoral Letters and Statements of the United States Catholic Bishops, Volume VI 1989–1997*, by the United States Conference of Catholic Bishops (USCCB) [Washington DC: USCCB, Inc., 1998], pages 417–418. Copyright © 1998 by the USCCB, Inc.)

8 How Can War Be Justified?

Overview

News of violence and war is, unfortunately, a daily part of life in our world. A day seldom goes by without media attention to the pain people inflict upon one another as individuals and nations. This session explores what it means to follow the way of peace and do God's will in an imperfect world. Participants will explore the concepts of nonviolence and just war as faith responses to the disregard for human dignity and human rights. The session closes with a prayer for peace and the challenge to make God's vision of peace a reality in our lives.

Outcomes

◆ The participants will come to appreciate God's vision of peace and the very real challenges involved in making that vision a reality in the world.
◆ The participants will be able to articulate the criteria used by the Church for judging a war to be just.
◆ The participants will be equipped to apply the principles of just war to current and potential international conflict in their world.

Background Reading

◆ This session covers chapter 26, pages 253–258, of *The Catholic Faith Handbook for Youth.*
◆ For further exploration, check out paragraph numbers 2302–2317 of the *Catechism.*
◆ Scriptural connections: Rom. 12:17–19 (mark of a true Christian), Eph. 6:10–17 (Be strong in the Lord.)
◆ *Catholic Youth Bible* article connections: "A Just War" (1 Mac., ch. 6), "Nonviolent Resistance" (2 Mac. 7:42), "I Will Sacrifice Myself" (2 Mac., ch. 7)

Core Session: How Can War Be Justified? (45 minutes)

◆ Involve: The Day Before the War Began (10 minutes)
◆ Explore: Reasons Enough for War (15 minutes)
◆ Reflect: Catholic Approaches to War and Peace (15 minutes)
◆ Pray: Praying for Peace (5 minutes)

Core Session: How Can War Be Justified? (45 minutes)

Preparation

- Gather the following items:
  - ❑ newsprint
  - ❑ markers
  - ❑ masking tape
  - ❑ sheets of blank paper, several for each participant
  - ❑ pens or pencils
  - ❑ copies of resource 7, "The Day Before the War Began," one for each small group

Involve: The Day Before the War Began (10 minutes)

1. Welcome the participants and introduce the topic in this way:

- This session explores war and the use of lethal force and how the Catholic faith approaches these issues. The topic is complex, but its importance makes it an essential issue to explore.
- Because of the topic's complexity, there are varying opinions and different approaches to this issue. It is important, however, that we approach topics such as war with a clear understanding of what the Church teaches. It is also important that we listen to and respect one another.
- I am going to read a series of war scenarios to you. Your task is to listen carefully to the scenario being read, think through the rationale offered, and decide whether war and the use of lethal force can reasonably be justified. If yes, why? If no, why not?

Distribute pens and paper, and encourage the participants to jot down their thoughts on each scenario. Note that there will be time for dialogue and sharing afterward.

2. Read through the scenarios found on resource 7, "The Day Before the War Began," one at a time. Allow a minute or so between the readings for the participants to reflect and write.

3. When you have finished reading each of the scenarios, go back and review each one with the participants. You will want to elicit their responses to the scenes and their reasons for deciding as they did.

Explore: Reasons Enough for War (15 minutes)

1. Organize the participants into small groups of three or four. Distribute newsprint and markers to each group. Say:

Try This

Instead of reading all the scenarios yourself, select and prepare participants to assist with this task. Varying voices will help participants hear and think about the scenarios differently.

- You are now ready for the second step in this process. When faced with the difficult task of deciding whether a war can be considered just, two things are essential from a Catholic perspective:
  ○ first, deciding whether the reasons for going to war are adequate, whether everything possible has been done to avoid or lessen the use of lethal force, and whether there is a likelihood of success.
  ○ second, even when the strict conditions needed to justify a declaration of war have been met, ongoing attention must be given to how the war is waged. There are necessary limits to how war is fought, both in weaponry and in strategy.
- The scenarios you just heard focused primarily on the first question, namely, the criteria for war to be justifiably declared.

Offer an example such as this: because war is justifiable only when undertaken for the right reason, it would be wrong to go to war for personal benefit.

2. Invite the small groups to take a deeper look at the issues raised by the war scenarios and to consider the limits that should be in place on how war is waged. To help them remember the scenarios, give a copy of resource 7, "The Day Before the War Began," to each small group. Provide the following instructions:

- In your small groups, discuss and then jot down on the newsprint your responses to the following open-ended sentences:
  ○ War can be justifiably declared only if . . .
  ○ As war is waged, the following needs to be true . . .

Allow 7 to 8 minutes for the groups to complete this task.

3. Ask one person from each group to post the responses on the wall. Invite all the participants to walk around and read the other groups' work. If time allows, invite participants to comment on what they see on the different sheets. Use the following questions:

- Where are the points of convergence?
- What are the most obvious differences?
- How difficult or easy do you think it is to declare a war "just" today? Why?

Reflect: Catholic Approaches to War and Peace (15 minutes)

1. Offer a short presentation on the Catholic approach to war and peace. Using the key points listed below, invite the participants to write down any questions or comments that come to mind as you speak. You might wish to note that the summary draws heavily on the 1993 U.S. Catholic Bishops' statement, *The Harvest of Justice Is Sown in Peace.*

- Central to the Judeo-Christian faith is belief in the God of peace. Through his life, death, and resurrection, Jesus has broken down the walls that divide people; he reconciles us with God and one another.
- The Spirit calls us to live in peace today, preparing the world for God's reign of justice, love, and peace.
- On a global scale, working for peace involves using government structures to defend human rights and promote the good of all the world's citizens: freeing people from poverty and the injustices that stifle human development, looking on all people as members of a single family, and working together to bring about justice and peace for all.
- In an imperfect and sinful world, conflict is inevitable. The Christian tradition offers two approaches to diminishing and defeating conflict: nonviolence and just war.
  - **Nonviolence** is a respected tradition in the Church. Christian nonviolence is deeply committed to eradicating injustice and defending human rights—but it chooses to do so through nonviolent means, such as dialogue and negotiation, protests and strikes, civil disobedience, and civilian resistance.
  - **Just War:** Like nonviolence, the Church's just war tradition begins with a strong presumption against the use of force. It then goes on to explain the conditions under which the presumption against force can be overridden to bring about a peace that honors and protects human dignity and human rights.
- Particular elements need to be in place to override the presumption against force and to justify entry into war. Seven criteria are offered:
  - Just Cause: Force may be used only to correct a massive violation of the rights of a large population.
  - Comparative Justice: Although rights and wrongs may exist on both sides of a conflict, the injustice suffered by one side must significantly outweigh that suffered by the other.
  - Legitimate Authority: Only duly constituted authorities may use deadly force or wage war.
  - Right Intention: Force may only be used in a just cause and solely for that purpose.
  - Probability of Success: Arms cannot be taken up if the cause is futile or if there is little likelihood of success without disproportionate and destructive measures.
  - Proportionality: The destruction expected from the use of force must be outweighed by the good that winning the war will achieve.
  - Last Resort: All peaceful alternatives must be tried before force can be applied.
- These criteria, taken as a whole, must be satisfied to override the presumption against force and to justify a declaration of war.

- The Catholic Church provides a moral framework for limiting the violence and regulating the use of force during armed conflict. Three criteria are offered:
  - Noncombatant Immunity: Civilian populations must not be targeted; attacks on military personnel or emplacements must avoid and minimize indirect or collateral harm to citizens.
  - Proportionality: Only the force militarily necessary should be employed in the conduct of hostilities. Disproportionate damage to civilian life and property is to be avoided.
  - Right Intention: Vengeance and indiscriminate violence are forbidden. Even in the midst of violence, warring leaders should work for a peace marked by justice and respect for the dignity of individuals and groups in society.
- In recent years, the Church's teaching on just war has helped shaped political dialogue about the viability of war and the use of force to settle international differences.
- The Church recognizes that Catholics and all people of conscience may have different approaches to bringing about a just and equitable peace.
- The Church believes that current world conditions, the neglect of peaceable virtues, and the destructive potential of today's weaponry demand ongoing dialogue on how modern war in all its savagery can meet the demanding criteria set by the just war tradition.
- Finally, Church teaching views the presence of Christians in the armed forces as a service to the common good and an exercise of the virtue of patriotism.
- At the same time, it urges legal protection for those who conscientiously refuse to participate in any war (conscientious objectors) and those who cannot in good conscience serve in conflicts they consider unjust or in ways that would require them to perform actions contrary to their deeply held moral convictions (selective conscientious objectors).
- Regardless of the path chosen, the Church calls on all people to remember and emulate the God of peace.

2. Once again, invite the participants to revisit the scenarios they heard earlier. Then ask the following question:
- Which of the principles you have just heard are embedded in the stories you were told earlier?

Revisit the scenarios one at a time, viewing them this time from the perspective of the related just war principles as follows:
- Scenario 1: Just Cause
- Scenario 2: Comparative Justice
- Scenario 3: Legitimate Authority
- Scenario 4: Right Intention

- Scenario 5: Probability of Success
- Scenario 6: Proportionality
- Scenario 7: Last Resort

3. Tell the participants the following:

- According to Church teaching, the intention to go to war would need to meet *all these criteria,* not just one, to be considered truly just.

Again, if time allows, ask participants to compare their group lists of the elements of a just war with the characteristics identified by Church teaching. Then ask them:

- Where do they find the greatest similarities?
- What is the greatest difference?

Pray: Praying for Peace (5 minutes)

Preparation

- Gather the following items:
  - ❑ copies of handout 8, "Prayer Attributed to Saint Francis," one for each participant
  - ❑ a cloth
  - ❑ a *Catholic Youth Bible* or other Bible
  - ❑ a cross
  - ❑ a pillar candle and matches
  - ❑ a basket
  - ❑ seasonal decorations
- Recruit and prepare a participant to read resource 8, "Pope John Paul II's World Day of Peace Message."
- Establish a prayer center in the space you will be using for this session. Cover a small table with a colorful cloth. Arrange a Bible, a cross, a candle, a basket, and any seasonal decoration you deem appropriate on the table. Put the prayer center where it will be visible during the session, allowing enough space around the table for participants to gather comfortably for prayer.

1. Begin the prayer by saying:

- This session has given you a lot to think about, perhaps leaving you wrestling with some deeply held convictions and some unanswered questions.
- It is important to continue struggling with these important questions in the days and weeks ahead. As you hear and read about violence and war in our world, keep the Church's teaching on war and peace in mind—and apply the criteria for a just war to existing and potential situations of international conflict.
- Our prayer today focuses us on peace. Let us take a moment to quiet ourselves.

Spirit & Song
connections

- ◆ "Be Not Afraid," by Bob Dufford, SJ
- ◆ "We Are the Light of the World," by Jean Anthony Greif and Tom Tomaszek

• I invite you to close your eyes, still your hearts, and imagine what the world would be like if the peace that God intends was a reality in our midst. How would people's lives be different? What would mark the relationships between individuals, groups, and former enemies? What feelings would rule people's hearts and minds?

Allow for a few moments of silence for quiet reflection.

2. Invite the participants to join in singing the gathering song you have chosen.

3. Invite the volunteer to read the excerpt from Pope John Paul II's World Day of Peace Message in resource 8. Allow a few moments of quiet reflection after the proclamation.

4. Distribute resource 8 and ask the participants to join in reciting the "Prayer Attributed to Saint Francis."

5. Invite the participants to share a greeting of peace with one another, and then challenge them to take that same spirit of peace home with them to share with family, friends, and all they meet in the coming days.

6. Conclude by inviting the participants to join in singing the closing song you have chosen.

The Day Before the War Began: Scenarios for Discussion

- Scenario 1

You are the democratically elected president of a small country in the Middle East. Unlike many of its neighbors, your country has been politically and economically stable for decades. Your economic stability rests on tourism and rug weaving. Taken together, they provide your people with a simple but adequate life. The quality of your rugs is known and appreciated internationally. Now the country immediately to the east is threatening your economic security. Its weavers have copied your rug patterns and technology and are turning out good-looking imitations at half the price. You know that your political party will go under if the economy declines—and everyone in the country will suffer. Moved by rug rage, you declare war on your eastern enemy.

- Scenario 2

The border situation between your country and a neighboring country to the north is a powder keg waiting to explode. Your country is rich in natural resources and controls the flow of water between the two nations. The drought of the past few years has left people in need on both sides of the border, but with fewer resources, your southern neighbor is clearly in more trouble than your country. Smugglers and illegal immigrants are destroying the fences along the border, evading the patrols, and making the surrounding area a scary place to live. In retaliation you have sent patrols across the border, trying to stem the illegal flow of immigrants into your country. There have been deaths and tragedies on both sides. Both countries are hurting, and neither is a clear winner in this conflict. You believe that things will only get worse in the future, so you declare war.

- Scenario 3

You are the leader of your country's armed forces. Your latest elected president is incapable of making decisions and is ignorant of the severe problems your country faces. You (and most military professionals) think action needs to be taken immediately to halt the flurry of terrorist attacks in your land. Fearing for your country's survival, you mobilize your forces and declare war on the terrorists. You will worry about the consequences after you have beaten your enemy and declared victory.

- Scenario 4

Two of your neighbors to the west are at war. So far, you have stayed neutral, but you are thinking of joining forces with one to conquer the other. Your country's population is expanding rapidly and will run out of living space soon. War will give you the opportunity to annex part of the loser's land, giving future generations a bit of breathing space. Without major loss of life or resources, you could end up the big winner in this war and help bring the conflict to a speedy close.

- Scenario 5

The neighboring country to your north is large and has been preparing for war for several years. Your army is outnumbered five to one, but your people are courageous and proud. When the war starts—and it is certain to come soon— you will encourage them to fight with all their strength rather than surrender to the forces sent their way. Being attacked is reason enough to fight to the death.

- Scenario 6

Your country has a long history of hatred with a neighboring country. Tension and intolerance increase every day. When war starts again, you know it will escalate quickly. Your country's shaky infrastructure (transportation and communication systems, health care and educational institutions) will be set back many years, and the environmental damage could take generations to repair. Damage to the enemy country, however, will be even worse. War is never pretty. People will suffer, but with your enemy soundly beaten, the violence should end for good.

- Scenario 7

When the tensions first flared, it looked like your country and the country with which you are in conflict could talk together and work out the problems. But now you know you cannot trust a thing they say. The other countries in your region have offered to intervene, but you figure that would just give your enemy time to strengthen defenses. You see little chance of resolving the conflict peacefully, so you decide, as the nation's leader, to initiate war while you still have a chance of getting the upper hand.

Pope John Paul II's World Day of Peace Message

Prayer for peace is not an afterthought to the work of peace. It is of the very essence of building the peace of order, justice, and freedom. To pray for peace is to open the human heart to the inroads of God's power to renew all things.

With the life-giving force of his grace, God can create openings for peace where only obstacles and closures are apparent; he can strengthen and enlarge the solidarity of the human family in spite of our endless history of division and conflict.

To pray for peace is to pray for justice, for a right ordering of relations within and among nations and peoples. It is to pray for freedom, especially for the religious freedom that is a basic human and civil right of every individual. To pray for peace is to seek God's forgiveness and to implore the courage to forgive those who have trespassed against us.

No peace without justice, no justice without forgiveness: this is what in this message I wish to say to believers and unbelievers alike, to all men and women of goodwill who are concerned for the good of the human family and for its future.

Reader: This is the teaching of our Church!

All: Thanks be to God.

(This excerpt is from Pope John Paul II's World Day of Peace Message, December 2001, numbers 14–15, at *www.usccb.org/pope/peacemessage.htm,* accessed July 17, 2003.)

Prayer Attributed to Saint Francis

Lord, make me an instrument of your peace,
Where there is hatred, let me sow love.
Where there is injury, pardon.
Where there is doubt, faith.
Where there is despair, hope.
Where there is darkness, light.
And where there is sadness, joy.

O Divine Master,
Grant that I may not so much seek to be consoled as to console,
To be understood as to understand,
To be loved as to love.
For it is in giving that we receive.
It is in pardoning that we are pardoned.
And it is in dying that we are born to eternal life.
Amen.

Hunger Among Us

Overview

Hunger remains a problem in our world and in our country. Despite the economic advances of the 1990s, people of all ages and families of every size and shape face hunger and malnutrition on a regular basis. Religious communities have taken the lead in responding to people's immediate needs by establishing thousands of food pantries, soup kitchens, and shelters, but a long-term solution is still needed. This session helps participants explore the reality of hunger, take an initial step toward being part of the solution, and learn options for where their concern can lead them.

Outcomes

◆ The participants will understand the meaning and real-life consequences of food insecurity and hunger.

◆ The participants will identify with the religious imperative to feed the hungry.

◆ The participants will commit to involvement in local efforts at hunger relief.

Background Reading

◆ For further exploration, check out paragraph numbers 1905–1912 of the *Catechism*.

◆ Scriptural connections: Isa. 58:6–8 (Share your bread with the hungry.), Mark 6:30–44 (Jesus feeds thousands.)

◆ *Catholic Youth Bible* article connections: "Give Food to the Hungry" (Tobit 4:16), "Hunger Pains" (Neh., ch. 5), "Food and Gratitude" (1 Cor. 10:23–33)

Core Session:
Hunger Among Us (65 minutes)

Preparation

- Gather the following items:
  - ❑ newsprint
  - ❑ markers
  - ❑ masking tape
  - ❑ sheets of blank paper, several for each participant
  - ❑ pens or pencils
  - ❑ copies of handout 9, "Hunger by the Numbers—A Quick Quiz," one for each participant
  - ❑ index cards, one for each participant
  - ❑ thin-line markers
  - ❑ 6-inch-by-2-inch construction paper strips, one for each participant
- Familiarize yourself with the hunger quiz and answer sheet.
- Using chapter 17, "Preparing Speakers and Panel Members to Educate Youth in Justice," select and prepare a local speaker. As you select and prepare the speaker, be clear about the particular focus of the presentation. Indicate that although you are interested in hearing about local needs and the work of this person's agency, you would like to use his or her presentation to help participants reflect on the faith dimensions of the issue. Accordingly, encourage the speaker to view the presentation as an act of witness to his or her faith. To help with this process, suggest that the speaker reflect on the following questions in preparation for the program:
  - ○ Why are you involved in ministering to the needs of the hungry?
  - ○ What does your faith have to do with it?
  - ○ Are there any scriptural images or passages that offer you support or direction in your service to the hungry?
  - ○ How has your involvement with the soup kitchen (or food pantry) affected your faith life? your view of others? the way you pray?
  - ○ When and where have you seen Jesus' presence in the kitchen or food line? in those who serve? in those who come for help?

  Emphasize with the speaker the power of real-life stories and personal witness in catching young people's attention and strengthening their religious convictions. Offer to assist with the development of his or her program presentation.
- Using one of the options listed in the Act: Responding to Local Hunger activity, select and prepare an appropriate action activity. The group's response to local hunger can take many different forms. Collecting food for the local soup kitchen or food pantry, raising funds through a program

like Catholic Relief Service's *Food Fast,* preparing part or all of a meal for a soup kitchen or shelter, or volunteering their time to assist with whatever task(s) the pantry, kitchen, or shelter needs done are all opportunities for the group to respond to the problem of hunger in your community. All of these, obviously, demand time and advance preparation. You can go into this session with a pre-selected action step or use the available session time to explore and decide on a particular approach with the group. In either case, the core session provides only enough time to get things started. You will need additional time to plan, prepare, and implement the action(s) you choose.

Involve: Foods I Really Like and Foods I Dislike (10 minutes)

1. Welcome the participants and introduce the session. Distribute paper and pens to the participants. Give these directions:

• Hold the paper lengthwise and draw a line across it, about a quarter of the way down.

Dislike	Really Like

• Write the words "Dislike" above the line on the far left and "Really Like" above the line on the far right.
• I will read a list of food items to you, one at a time. As you hear each item, write it below the line where it fits on your personal food preference list. Do you dislike this food (despise it, wouldn't eat it if it were the last morsel on earth), or do you really like this food (awesome taste, could eat it every day for life)?
• If the item is something you have not heard of or tasted before, put it where you think it fits, given your preferences and your usual approach to new food challenges.

Suggest the items listed below. You may add to or subtract from the list.

• spaghetti and meatballs
• warm spinach salad
• liver and onions
• hot dog with sauerkraut
• fried chicken
• tortilla chips and salsa
• asparagus
• Hawaiian pizza with ham and pineapple
• black bean soup
• grapefruit
• oysters on the half shell (raw, of course)
• goat meat stew

- hunks of blue cheese on whole wheat crackers
- sour cream and onion potato chips
- baked potato with all the fixings
- Now add a food item of your own to your list at each edge of the sheet
  . . . a food you dislike and one you really like.

2. Give the participants a couple of minutes to compare their lists with the youth around them. Then elicit responses to this question:

- What do you do when you are at home or visiting friends for dinner and the food set before you falls more into the hate than the love end of your preferences?

Participants' responses to this question will most likely include the following:

- complain about an existing upset stomach and decide "regretfully" to go without
- nibble a little, leave a lot
- hide it in your napkin when no one is looking
- feed it to the dog
- ask for a bowl of cereal instead
- make a peanut butter and jelly sandwich
- rush off immediately after the meal for a fast food fix

3. In closing, say something like:

- Everyone has personal food preferences, and as different as they may be, as a group we probably have a couple of things in common—the certainty that there will be food available when we need it and the ability to find something to eat if what's being served is not to our liking.

Explore: Hunger by the Numbers (10 minutes)

1. Explain that you would like to start this segment of the program by describing a phrase that the participants hear a lot when they start to explore the reality of hunger and need in our country. The phrase is "food security." Ask the participants what they think the term means. Then offer the following description:

- *Food security* entails living with a fair degree of certainty about when and where your next meal will be and how you will get it. There is a sense, too, that the mix and quality of the food will be as healthy as the quantity. Food security is about having *enough* of the *right kind* of food.
- People who are "food insecure" may not know where their next meal is coming from or (even if they eat regularly) may be going without the kind of food needed for healthy growth and development. Either of these paths can quickly lead to malnutrition and hunger.

2. Organize the participants into groups of three to four people. Give each participant a copy of handout 9, "Hunger by the Numbers—A Quick Quiz." Then offer the following explanation:

- The questions on the sheet deal with hunger in the United States and provide a clear picture of how significant the issue of hunger is in our country.
- Read through the questions together in your small group, and come up with your best guess at the appropriate answer.

3. After allowing ample time for deliberation, review the questions and answers with them, using this answer key:

- Question One: **Disagree.** The number of people who are food insecure is still on the rise. More people than ever before are using soup kitchens and food pantries to supplement their food needs.
- Question Two: **D.** In 2001 more than thirty-three million people lived with food insecurity.
- Question Three: **Disagree.** Hunger and poverty aren't just urban problems. Of the country's food aid recipients, more than 32 percent live in the suburbs and 15 percent in rural areas. Roughly half of the country's hungry people live outside the central city.
- Question Four: **C.** Almost 12 percent (11.7 percent) of the U.S. population is living in poverty.
- Question Five: **Agree.** The child poverty rate for rural areas is 18.9 percent—almost 1 in every 5 children. In metro areas the rate is 15.4 percent—less than 1 in 6.
- Question Six: **C.** Almost 39 percent of the people served by America's Second Harvest (the country's largest food relief organization) are children under the age of 18. An additional 11 percent are senior citizens. Together, these two vulnerable groups make up half the people receiving food assistance from pantries and soup kitchens.
- Question Seven: **Agree.** Although a high school diploma will not guarantee a steady job and food security, it does make them more likely. Less than two-thirds of the population served by hunger relief charities earned a high school diploma or equivalent degree, compared to 84 percent of the general U.S. population.
- Question Eight: **B.** The federal poverty level for a family of three in 2001 was defined as $14,630. Families with one wage earner at the current minimum wage would not make nearly this amount.

(The questions and answers come from "Hunger in America 2001," a research report compiled by America's Second Harvest. For additional information and updated statistics, visit the organization online at *www.secondharvest.org./whoshungry/hunger_study_intro.html.*)

4. After the review, invite the group to discuss the following questions:

- Is the reality of hunger different from how you had originally pictured it?
- Which of the statements did you find hardest to believe?
- What motivates you the most to want to do something to solve the problem of hunger among us?

Reflect: Soup Served in Jesus' Name: Witness to Faith (20 minutes)

1. Introduce this part of the session by providing the following information to the participants:

- America's Second Harvest recently published a comprehensive report on hunger in the United States. America's Second Harvest, which has a network of more than 200 food banks and food rescue programs, provides assistance to more than twenty-three million hungry Americans each year by distributing over 1.5 billion pounds of food to individuals and families in need.
- One finding of their study points to the active involvement of religious groups in responding to the hunger among us. They report that three-quarters of the country's food pantries and soup kitchens (76 percent and 71 percent) and almost half (43 percent) of its shelters are run by faith-based agencies affiliated with churches, mosques, synagogues, and other religious organizations!
- These statistics speak volumes about the Church's concern for the hungry and the ways in which people express their religious beliefs in action.

(These statistics are from "Hunger in America 2001," by America's Second Harvest. The report is available online at *www.secondharvest.org/whoshungry/hunger_study_intro.html.*)

2. Introduce the speaker, emphasizing that this segment of the program will focus on the call of our faith to feed the hungry. Use these or similar comments:

- Today's speaker will give some background on local hunger and the work that he or she does, but the primary focus will be on how the work is viewed through the eyes of faith, a living expression of Catholic beliefs and values.

Distribute index cards and pens to the participants. Invite them to jot down any questions that occur to them during the presentation. Let them know that a brief question-and-answer period will follow the presentation. Then welcome the presenter.

3. Follow the presentation with a chance for questions and dialogue with the speaker. You can do this by collecting the questions the participants have noted on their index cards and selecting a few or by inviting the participants to ask any questions they might have.

4. Thank the speaker for the willingness to be with you, the active witness to faith and involvement in the group's action response to local hunger.

Act: Responding to Local Hunger (5 minutes)

1. Select one of the following approaches to use with the participants.

- **Option 1.** Indicate that there are various ways in which the group can respond to the issue of local hunger. Invite the participants to brainstorm possibilities with you, or present a variety of options for them to choose from, using descriptions of the actual needs of groups and service agencies in your area or other possibilities such as collecting food for the local soup kitchen or volunteering time at a food pantry. Involve participants in considering the pros and cons, benefits and requirements of each option. Record on newsprint the opportunities raised and thoughts shared. Select an appropriate action response together, and set a time to meet for further planning and preparation.

- **Option 2.** Present an overview of an action response you have selected in advance, for example, collecting boxes of food basics to provide families with three or four simple meals. Involve young people in the initial planning for the project, such as selecting menus and deciding whether the project will be strictly for the group or a family or parish-wide undertaking. As time allows, develop a project schedule, outline leadership roles, and brainstorm possible approaches to raising the needed funds. Establish a time to meet for continued planning and preparation.

Pray: Use Us, God, for the Works of Service (20 minutes)

Preparation

- Gather the following items:
  - ❑ a cloth
  - ❑ a *Catholic Youth Bible* or other Bible
  - ❑ a cross
  - ❑ a pillar candle and matches
  - ❑ a round tray
  - ❑ copies of handout 10, "Use Us, God, for the Works of Service," one for each participant
- Select a gathering and closing song with the theme of feeding the poor.
- Establish a prayer center in the space you will be using for this session. Cover a small table with a colorful cloth. Arrange a Bible, a cross, a candle, a round tray, and colored construction paper strip on the table. Put the prayer center where it will be visible during the session, allowing enough space around the table for participants to gather comfortably for prayer.
- Recruit a reader to proclaim Matt. 25:31–45.

Spirit & Song
connections

- ◆ "Bread for the World," by Bernadette Farrell
- ◆ "Pescador de Hombres/ Lord, You Have Come," by Cesáreo Gabaráin

1. Gather the participants around the prayer center. Distribute handout 10, "Use Us, God, for the Works of Service," as well as a thin-line marker and strip of construction paper to each participant. Invite the participants to join in singing the gathering song you have selected.

2. Invite the reader to come forward and proclaim Matt. 25:31–45. Ask the participants to listen for a word or phrase that stands out for them. Allow a few minutes for quiet reflection.

3. As a response to the reading, tell the participants they will make a bookmark to give to another participant. Give these instructions:

- As you listened to the Scripture reading from Matthew, what did you hear? What words spoke to you?
- I invite you to make a bookmark that will be a reminder of our session today and a challenge to make a difference in our community by reaching out to those in need.
- On your bookmark, write the word or phrase you heard most clearly in the Scripture reading. Next to that word or phrase, write a short prayer or hope for the person who will get the bookmark, that he or she will be encouraged to reach out to those in need. When you are finished with your bookmark, place it on the tray on our prayer table.

Allow a few minutes for the participants to complete this task.

4. Distribute handout 10 and invite the participants to pray together "Use Us, God, for the Works of Service."

5. Take the tray of bookmarks around the room, inviting the participants to select one. Encourage them to read their bookmark each day in the coming week and to choose one thing they can do to make a difference.

6. Conclude the prayer experience by inviting the participants to join in singing the closing song you have selected.

Hunger by the Numbers— A Quick Quiz

Circle the response you think best fits the question. Be ready to explain why you think your answer is correct.

1. Hunger and *food insecurity* in the United States are still a problem, but with our improving economy, there are fewer hungry people in our country every year.

   Agree   **Disagree**

2. In 2001 how many people were *food insecure*—hungry or worried about where their next meal would come from?

   A. 5,000,000   **B.** 10,000,000   **C.** 20,000,000   **D.** 30,000,000

3. The country's hunger problem is predominantly an urban, central-city problem. There are not many hungry people living in the suburbs or in rural areas.

   Agree   **Disagree**

4. How many Americans are living in poverty?

   A. 4%   **B.** 8%   **C.** 12%   **D.** 16%   **E.** 20%

5. Child poverty rates are higher in rural areas than in metropolitan areas.

   Agree   **Disagree**

6. What percentage of the people who use food pantries and soup kitchens are children or senior citizens?

   A. 20% (1/5)   **B.** 33% (1/3)   **C.** 50% (1/2)   **D.** 75% (3/4)

7. Getting a high school diploma makes it less likely that a person will need food assistance.

   Agree   **Disagree**

8. According to the U.S. government, how much annual income does a family of three need to avoid living in poverty?

   A. $11,245   **B.** $14,630   **C.** $17,853   **D.** $21,290

Note: The questions and answers come from the research compiled by America's Second Harvest. For additional information and updated statistics, visit America's Second Harvest online at *www.secondharvest.org*.

Use Us, God, for the Works of Service

God, Creator and Source of the good things in life,

Make us aware of how blessed we are:

In family and friends who reach out and care.

In the abundance of resources we're given to share.

For homes of our own and regular meals.

For the clothes in our closets—probably more than we need!

For school and for work and the chance to make choices.

For all that we have and are able to do.

Help us see these things for what they are—your gifts to us—

And to share them with others—as your gifts to them.

Use us, Father, for the works of service

To befriend the lonely, house the homeless,

And feed the hungry in our midst.

We ask this in the name of Jesus,

Friend of the Lost,

Shelter for the Poor,

And Bread of Life,

And in the Holy Spirit,

Amen.

Part C

Justice Retreats and Extended Sessions

Responding in Service to the Needs of the Poor:
An Overnight Retreat Experience

Overview

Pockets of poverty exist in even the wealthiest cities of our country. Whether obvious or hidden from view, poverty saps the energy of the poor and leaves everyone in society poorer because of its presence among us. This retreat experience helps participants understand the causes and the consequences of poverty for individuals and society and respond in faithful service to the needs of poor people.

Outcomes

◆ The participants will be able to distinguish between the concepts of relative and absolute poverty and to talk knowledgeably about the causes and the consequences of poverty for individuals and families in need in their community.

◆ The participants will connect more deeply with the person of Jesus and with his compassion for people in need.

◆ The participants will reflect on the role of service in their lives and consider options for their ongoing involvement in the lives of individuals and families in need.

Overall Preparation

Besides the usual preparation for retreats, such as arranging for team, site, meals, and logistics, this retreat requires two important aspects of advance preparation. First, you will need to select appropriate service site where participants can work during the second day of the retreat. Secondly, you will be recruiting and preparing a panel of speakers for session 3. You will find help with this preparation and other aspects of this retreat in the Strategies section (part D) of this manual.

AT A GLANCE

Day One

7:30 p.m. Arrival, Welcome, and Introductions

8:00 p.m. Session One: Community Building

8:30 p.m. Opening Prayer: In the Presence of God

8:45 p.m. Session Two: The Meaning of Poverty: Relative and Absolute

9:30 p.m. Snack Break, Games, Music, Quiet Recreation

10:30 p.m. Evening Prayer: Thankfulness for God's Abundance

11:00 p.m. Lights Out

Day Two

7:00 a.m. Rise

7:30 a.m. Breakfast

8:15 a.m. Morning Prayer: Walking with Jesus

8:30 a.m. Session Three: Poverty in Our Area, A Panel Presentation

9:30 a.m. Break

10:00 a.m. Session Four: Jesus and the Poor

11:00 a.m. Break

11:15 a.m. Travel, Final Preparation for Service, Lunch

12:00 m. Session Five: Serving the Needs of the Poor

117

Retreat Outline
Day One

7:30 p.m. Arrival, Welcome, and Introductions

Preparation

- Gather the following items:
  - ❏ name tags
  - ❏ pens or pencils
- Post a program schedule in the meeting, dining, and sleeping areas.

1. As participants arrive, greet them, show them to the registration area, and invite them to make a name tag.

2. Once everyone has gathered, welcome them to the retreat. Offer a brief introduction to the facility. Introduce the program staff, and let participants know who the point person is for particular activities—programs, food, prayer and music, sleeping accommodations, contact with home, emergencies, and so forth. Offer the participants an opportunity to share their names and their hopes for the retreat.

3. Provide the participants with an overview of the retreat schedule and experience. Inform them that there will be a mix of activities and time for both personal reflection and group interaction. Explain that the schedule will work if people help one another be on time. Respond to any immediate questions participants have.

4. Review the ground rules for the program. These may include information on off-limit areas in the facility, expected behavior during the retreat experience, encouragement to share and mix, keeping an open mind, and focusing on the opportunity offered by the present moment. List the tasks you will need assistance with during the retreat (like meal preparation and cleanup, prayer leading, and music).

8:00 p.m. Session One: Community Building

Begin with a community builder to help the participants get to know one another. When the community builder is finished, invite participants to join in prayer around the table.

8:30 p.m. Opening Prayer: In the Presence of God

Preparation

- Gather the following items:
  - ❏ a *Catholic Youth Bible* or other Bible
  - ❏ a cloth
  - ❏ a cross
  - ❏ a pillar candle and matches
  - ❏ thematic symbols or seasonal decorations
- Select a gathering song and a concluding song with the theme of discipleship. Possibilities include "To You, O God, I Lift Up My Soul," by Bob Hurd; "God's Love Is Everlasting," by Tom Tomaszek; "Thy Word Is a Lamp," by Michael W. Smith and Amy Grant; "We Are the Light of the World," by Jean Anthony Greif and Tom Tomaszek.
- Establish a prayer center in the presentation area or in a space of its own. Cover a small table with a colorful cloth. Arrange a Bible, a cross, a candle, and any thematic symbols or seasonal decorations you deem appropriate on the table.
- Recruit a reader to proclaim Luke 4:16–21.

1. Invite the participants to join in singing the gathering song you have chosen.

2. Share the following with the participants:
- I invite you to place yourselves consciously in the presence of the God who is always with you—in moments of happiness and joy, challenge and struggle, doubt and uncertainty.

After a moment's silence, pray the following:
- Thank you, God, for your ongoing presence in our lives and for the chance to be here together. Help us keep our hearts and minds open to what we hear and experience. Help us live our lives as faithful disciples of Jesus, sharing who we are and what we have with those in need. We ask this in the name of the Father and of the Son and of the Holy Spirit. Amen.

3. Invite the reader to come forward and proclaim Luke 4:16–21: Jesus proclaims his mission. Allow a few moments for quiet reflection.

4. Offer a brief reflection that includes the following points:
- We come together as group of people who are uniquely gifted and who share the belief that God is present to us in times of joy and trouble.
- As a child of God and disciple of Jesus, each of us brings a unique gift to our time together today and to tomorrow's service with the poor.
- The passage from Luke's Gospel tells us how Jesus saw his mission in life—and offers a glimpse of what following Jesus means for us today.

3:00 p.m. Break
3:30 p.m. Reflection and Evaluation
4:30 p.m. Celebrating Service

- Let us use this time together to hear what God has to tell us about the gifts we have been given, as well as the needs of the people who live around us. In the process, we hope to learn more about what it means to follow Jesus as young disciples.

5. Invite the participants to join in praying the Lord's Prayer.

6. Ask the participants to respond to each of the following prayers with the phrase "Be with us."

As we honor the God of heaven and earth, we pray . . .

As we work with Jesus to make God's will known and the Kingdom a reality today, we pray . . .

As we recognize that everything we have is a gift from God and as we share our lives with others, we pray . . .

As we grow in confidence of God's love and forgiveness and as we pardon those who have hurt us, we pray . . .

We ask this in the name of God, whose power and glory lives on forever and ever.

Amen.

7. Bring the prayer to a close with a greeting of peace. Invite the participants to join in singing the closing song you have chosen.

8:45 p.m. Session Two: The Meaning of Poverty, Relative and Absolute

Preparation
- Gather the following items:
  - ❏ newsprint
  - ❏ markers
  - ❏ masking tape
  - ❏ construction paper in various colors
  - ❏ sheets of blank paper, several for each participant
  - ❏ pens or pencils
- Using construction paper and markers, make the following four signs: Very Poor, Somewhat Needy, Slightly Better Off, and Wealthy. Post the signs in different corners of the room.
- Familiarize yourself with the activity, which works best in a large area cleared of chairs.

1. Explain that the opening session begins with a Four Corners activity. Say something like the following:
- For this activity, everyone stands in the center of the room. I will read a statement. You will respond to the statement by moving to the sign posted in the room that best represents your viewpoint.

2. Gather participants in the center of the room. One at a time, read through the statements listed below. After each statement is read, invite the participants to move to the sign that best represents their response. Ask questions about why the participants chose as they did. Encourage them to identify the reasoning behind their choice. Then invite the participants to return to the center of the room to listen to the next statement.

- My family has a television in every room of the house—except for the bathroom and dining room.
- I am happy to own two pairs of shoes—one for school and one for play.
- I never worry about when or where my next meal will be.
- No one in our house has a cell phone . . . in fact, we do not have phone service at all.
- I'm counting on a computer for my next birthday and Internet service soon after.
- I am afraid of what will happen to me every time I step outside my front door.
- My favorite family vacation was a weeklong trip to Disney World.
- Half my clothes are hand-me-downs from other family members.
- We are lucky; we have family medical insurance, even if it does not cover eye care or trips to the dentist.
- If I make it out of high school, I would like to learn a trade so I will have a steady income.
- I have a credit card of my own, and my parents handle all the payments.

3. Following the activity, instruct participants to sit down. Then lead them in a discussion about the experience. Use questions such as:

- What was the overall experience like for you?
- When was the decision about where to stand easiest for you? When was the decision most difficult?
- Did all the questions really relate to poverty? Why or why not?
- What statement or response from the group most surprised you? Why?

4. Note that as you watch the activity unfold, several thoughts come to mind. In addition to your own observations, you might say:

- One thought is about the different elements or expressions of poverty. Usually when we think of poverty, we think about the lack of physical things like food, clothing, or shelter. But this activity focused on other things: how important it is to feel safe where you live or believing that you have at least moderate control over decisions about your life.
- A second thought has to do with the "relativity" of poverty. No matter how rich or poor we are, there is always somebody who has more or less than we do. It is equally clear that as relative as poverty may be, there is also a sharp divide between people who have enough to spare and people who do not have even the basics needed to survive and grow. Living without

the basics, lacking one or more of the services required for a healthy life, is sometimes referred to as "absolute poverty."

5. Ask the group to name the basics of life. Remind them that the lack of basics moves people into the realm of absolute poverty. List the participants' responses on newsprint. Then ask where they think their community, in general, fits on the poverty to wealth scale:

- Is our community relatively poorer or wealthier than the surrounding towns?
- How does life here compare with life in other parts of the United States? How does it compare with life in other parts of the world?

6. Close the session with a discussion using these questions:

- Does absolute poverty exist right here in our community?
- If so, whom does it touch? Which of life's essentials are they missing?
- What do you think life is like for them?

9:30 p.m. Snack Break, Games, Music, Quiet Recreation

Encourage participants to mix and talk or to take time for personal reflection and journaling. Use board games that encourage sharing and/or teamwork. Keep the music upbeat and nonintrusive.

10:30 p.m. Evening Prayer: Thankfulness for God's Abundance

Preparation

- Gather the following items:
  - ❑ a *Catholic Youth Bible* or other Bible
  - ❑ a basket of fruit
- Select a gathering song and a closing song with a theme of thankfulness. Possibilities include "Seek Ye First," by Karen Lafferty; "Rain Down," by Jaime Cortez; "Malo! Malo! Thanks Be to God," by Jesse Manibusan; "We Are the Light," by Jesse Manibusan.
- Recruit a reader to proclaim 1 Chron. 29:10–14.

1. Distribute copies of the hymnal to each participant. Then invite them to join in singing the opening song you have chosen.

2. Invite the reader to come forward and proclaim 1 Chron. 29:10–14. Allow a few moments for quiet reflection. Then ask the participants to reflect on these questions:

- Where do you find God's blessings in your life?
- What has God given you to share with others?

3. Say to the participants:

- Let us bring our gratitude as well as our concerns and worries to God this evening. I invite you to offer an intention or petition, and we will respond by saying, "Your abundant love fills us with hope."

Invite the young people to share their thoughts in prayer. At the end of the prayers of intercession, invite the participants to pray the Lord's Prayer together.

4. Invite the participants to join in singing the sending forth song you have chosen.

11:00 p.m. Lights Out

Day Two

7:00 a.m. Rise

7:30 a.m. Breakfast

After breakfast, have participants put together sack lunches to take with them to the work site.

8:15 a.m. Morning Prayer: Walking with Jesus

Preparation

- Gather the following items:
  - ❏ a *Catholic Youth Bible* or other Bible
  - ❏ construction paper in various colors, one sheet for each participant
  - ❏ pens or thin-line markers, one for each participant
- Select a gathering song and a closing song with the theme of service. Possibilities include "City of God," by Dan Schutte; "What Is Our Service to Be," by Delores Dufner and Scot Crandal; "Strength for the Journey," by Michael John Poirier; "This Little Light of Mine," traditional spiritual.
- Recruit a reader to proclaim Matt. 9:35–38.

1. Gather together around the prayer table, and distribute copies of the hymnals to each participant. Invite them to join in singing the gathering song you have chosen.

2. Invite the reader to come forward and proclaim Matt. 9:35–38. Allow a few moments for quiet reflection. Then ask the participants to reflect on these questions:

- What does it mean to be a disciple of Jesus?
- How is Jesus calling you to serve poor and needy people today?

3. Distribute construction paper and pens to the participants. Give these instructions:

- On the construction paper, trace the outline either of your hand or of your shoe. As you recall the words from Matthew's Gospel and your own reflection on how Jesus calls you to serve poor and needy people, write those words on your paper hand or foot.

Allow a few minutes for the participants to accomplish this task. Then invite them to share one thing they wrote on their construction paper.

4. Close the prayer by inviting the participants to join in singing the sending forth song you have chosen.

8:30 a.m. Session Three: Poverty in Our Area, A Panel Presentation

Note. Chapter 17 of this manual provides information about selecting and preparing speakers and panel members. You will want to limit the panel to three or four speakers. Be sure to include a speaker from the group or agencies you will be assisting later in the day. This will help participants make a direct connection between their learning and consequent actions.

Preparation

- Gather the following items:
  - ❑ index cards, one for each participant
  - ❑ pens or pencils

1. Summarize the group's learning from the prior session. Recall their insights about relative and absolute poverty and their knowledge of or questions about local poverty.

2. Explain the format of the session:

- We will hear a brief presentation by each panel member, followed by a break and the opportunity for questions and dialogue with the speakers.
- Each of you will receive an index card. Please jot down any questions that come to mind during the speakers' presentations. I will give you a minute or two to write any initial questions you may have.

3. Introduce the speakers, and facilitate the presentation process. When the panelists have finished speaking, collect the participants' question cards, and call a brief break. During the break, read the question cards. Let the speakers know about any question that is directed to them personally or to their agency. Call the participants back together, and facilitate the question-and-answer process. Keep the dialogue as informal and conversational as possible, allowing time for comments and additional questions from participants.

4. To close the session, thank the panelists for their participation and the participants for their attention and thoughtful questions.

9:30 a.m. Break

10:00 a.m. Session Four: Jesus and the Poor

Preparation
- Gather the following items:
  - ❑ blank paper, a few sheets for each small group
  - ❑ pens or pencils
  - ❑ *Catholic Youth Bibles* or other Bibles, one for each participant
  - ❑ simple props and costume pieces for use in the team skits (optional)

1. Organize the participants into groups of four to six. Assign or ask each group to select a facilitator and a recorder. Share with the participants the following scenario and task:

- **The Scenario:** It is the second year of Jesus' active ministry. The members of your small group are among his earliest followers. A new and younger group of followers is ready to make a commitment to Jesus' teaching and way of life. They are high on energy but fairly low on experience. Your team has been given the job of sharing the history of the past year with them and helping them better understand what Jesus' life and mission are all about. A particular focus of your task is to help them adopt Jesus' attitude toward poor people, a stance in stark contrast to society's approach. His compassion for those in need is obvious in both the stories he tells and his daily contact with people in need.

- **The Task:** Your job is to help these new followers adopt Jesus' mindset toward poor people. You will want to handle this task creatively. You have decided to sit together and identify the highlights of Jesus' attitude and action toward poor people. Then you will choose one of the stories, teachings, or events and act it out in a way that your young audience will appreciate.

Give the small groups 20 to 30 minutes to accomplish this task. Offer Bibles to each small group to help them in the "remembering" process. Be available to answer questions or to help them find the supplies they need for their presentation. Let them know that sharing will involve two parts: a summary of their discussion on Jesus' treatment of poor people and a dramatic presentation of the particular story, teaching, or event they have decided to highlight.

2. Invite each group to come forward to present its discussion summary and skit. When the presentations are finished, ask and then discuss with the participants the following questions:
- What consistent themes did you see in each presentation?

- What do the presentations, taken together, tell us about Jesus' attitude toward poor and vulnerable people?
- What are the implications of Jesus' attitude and actions for his followers?

Then offer the following comments:

- I am going to share a short reading with you to emphasize the importance of the concept of compassion for the poor. The reading is taken from *Economic Justice for All,* the 1986 pastoral letter of the U.S. Conference of Catholic Bishops on Catholic social teaching and the nation's economy.
- In the introduction, the bishops describe the basic moral principles on which the letter is based. One of their principles proclaims that *all members of society have a special obligation to the poor and vulnerable.* They write:

> From the Scriptures and Church teaching, we learn that the justice of a society is tested by the treatment of the poor. The justice that was the sign of God's covenant with Israel was measured by how the poor and unprotected—the widow, the orphan, and the stranger—were treated. . . . Throughout Israel's history and in early Christianity, the poor are agents of God's transforming power. "The Spirit of the Lord is upon me, therefore he has anointed me. He has sent me to bring good tidings to the poor" (Luke 4:18). . . . Jesus takes the side of those most in need. In the Last Judgment, so dramatically described in St. Matthew's Gospel, we are told that we will be judged according to how we respond to the hungry, the thirsty, the naked, the stranger. As followers of Christ, we are challenged to make a fundamental "option for the poor"—to speak for the voiceless, to defend the defenseless, to assess life styles, policies, and social institutions in terms of their impact on the poor. This "option for the poor" does not mean pitting one group against another, but rather, strengthening the whole community by assisting those who are most vulnerable. As Christians, we are called to respond to the needs of *all* our brothers and sisters, but those with the greatest need require the greatest response.
>
> (USCCB, *Economic Justice for All,* no. 16.)

After reading the bishops' words, continue by saying:

- The bishops' statement remains as powerful and challenging today as it was when first written. Making an "option for the poor and vulnerable" part of our lives day in and day out is quite a task, but one that can be very rewarding.
- The time and energy we are devoting to learning, prayer, and service during this retreat are just a few of the many ways of expressing an "option for the poor and vulnerable," walking with Jesus today in service to those in need.

11:00 a.m. Break

11:15 a.m. Travel, Final Preparation for Service, Lunch

Note. Final preparation can take place just prior to leaving for the service site or upon arrival, whichever works best for you and the service site. Depending on the work site, travel distance, and type of work, participants can eat lunch on the way or at the work site.

12:00 m. Session Five: Serving the Needs of the Poor

The retreat program culminates with service to those in need locally. For effectiveness, service incorporates four distinct tasks: preparation, engagement in service, reflection, and celebration. With the advance planning and preparation handled prior to the retreat and the justice focus built into the retreat, most of the preparation has been completed. Now it is time for immediate preparation and engagement in service.

Preparation involves participants in four tasks:

- learning about the issues they will encounter at the work site
- reflecting on the issues from a faith perspective
- becoming familiar and comfortable with the service site and what they are likely to encounter there
- getting the training and skills they need to accomplish the tasks they will be doing

Participants should be knowledgeable about local poverty and aware of the importance of a faith response to the needs of the poor and vulnerable. They may need, however, to know a bit more about where they will be working and what they can expect to encounter. The more comfortable they are with the program site, the better prepared they will be to focus their energy and effort on real service. Depending on what they have been asked to do, participants may also need some prior direction or training. Their concerns here may focus on the people being served (who they are, whether it is okay to talk with them, if there are questions or topics they should avoid). They could also be concerned about the task (if they will be working by themselves or with their friends, what if the clients do not like the meal they are serving, and so on). If participants are nervous about the service they have been asked to do, a brief overview by an agency staff member or a regular volunteer will usually allay their fears.

You can do a variety of things to help make the service experience a rousing success:

- Check in regularly with participants. Ask how they are doing and if there is anything you can do to help things go more smoothly.
- Provide enthusiastic support, affirmation, and a break if needed. Listen to stories and insights. Give participants a drink or snack.

- Run interference as necessary. If more supplies are needed or there is a question they cannot answer, volunteer to find what they need. Convert "problems" into opportunities for learning and growth.
- Explore what else your group could do on-site, either during this visit or in the future.
- Help young people balance doing and relating on-site. If they are in the middle of a task and are invited to join in conversation, let them know that this is a good thing. Invite them to take the initiative to start a conversation.
- Jot down or make mental notes of the things you do not want to forget about the day's experience. Encourage the young people to do the same. You will both appreciate this extra effort when it is time to reflect on the day's experiences.
- Get involved if your help is needed and asked for. Make the service activity enjoyable. Encourage a sense of humor and the ability to laugh at oneself.

3:00 p.m. Break

3:30 p.m. Reflection and Evaluation

Building reflection and evaluation time into the retreat allows participants to learn from one another and to put the day's events into a larger faith context. It also serves as a bridge to future service involvement, at the same site or in a different location that offers other challenges and opportunities for growth. Consider the following approaches for helping young people reflect on their service experience.

- Start unpacking the day's experience during the ride back to the retreat location. Listening to the "car talk" will give you some initial feedback on the day's events.
- Schedule a formal time to discuss and evaluate the service experience after participants have had a chance to catch their breath, get a snack, and expel a bit of their pent-up energy. Let participants know that "unpacking" the experience is an important part of the overall service package.
- Start by looking at "the way things were" where they were, whom they met, what happened, and how they felt about it. Share the stories.
- Consider "the way things are." What did the day's experience teach them about the reality of the issues they looked at earlier in the retreat? Does it look or feel any different now than before they arrived? Did they learn anything new about the size or shape, causes or consequences of poverty and need?
- Explore "the way things should be." What beliefs or values came into play at the work site? Which are being honored? Which are being rejected?

What needs to change to make things more the way they should be on-site and with the particular issue in general?

- Ponder "the ways they have grown through the experience." What has the experience taught them about themselves? their talents and gifts? the things that excite and energize them? their impact on others?
- Finally, ask whether they would do it this way again. Evaluate how the project played out for them. Was the timing right? Was the task worth doing? Did they feel that their presence was appreciated? Is it worth doing again, perhaps on a regular basis? How could things be done better next time around?
- Make the faith dimension explicit. Ask participants where faith came into the experience or what God is teaching them about themselves through the experience. How was Jesus present with them during the day's events? What do they think he would say to them at day's end? What would they like to explore and experience next as they walk with Jesus in service to poor people?

Allow ample time for group reflection. Encourage participants to continue to think through their learnings and to share their thoughts and reflections with their family and friends. Encourage them to take their thoughts to prayer, thanking God for the experience and the people they met and asking God's assistance in whatever tasks might be in store for them in the future.

4:30 p.m. Celebrating Service

Preparation

- Gather the following items:
  ☐ *Catholic Youth Bibles* or other Bibles, one for each of the four readers
- Recruit four readers to proclaim Matt. 25:31–34, 25:35–36, 25:37–39, 25:40.
- Select a gathering song and a concluding song with the theme of going forth to serve. Possibilities include "Pescador de Hombres/Lord, You Have Come," by Cesáreo Gabarain; "We Are the Light of the World," by Jean Anthony Greif; "The Call," by Tom Franzak.
- Post a sheet of newsprint near the prayer table after having written the following phrase on it:
  ☐ May you be blessed for being the hands and feet of Jesus today.

1. Distribute hymnals to the participants. Tell the young people:
- The retreat is coming to a close, but we want to take time to honor the work we have done for others.

Invite them to come together in prayer by first centering themselves and focusing on God, who gave them the hands and feet with which they served today. After a few moments of silence, encourage participants to lift their minds, bodies, and hearts to God by singing the gathering song you have chosen.

2. Invite the four volunteers to come forward to proclaim Matt. 25:31–40. Allow a few moments of silence.

3. Share with the participants:

- As a response to God's word, let us lift up in prayer those whom we met today who need us to be the hands and feet of Jesus in their lives, those who need food or shelter, clothing or liberation from fear.
- Hold your hands up, join them together with the palms up, and symbolically place the people you encountered today in God's hands. If you would like, quietly speak the first names of those special people for whom you wish us to pray.

Allow sufficient time for anyone who wishes to name someone. Then say:

- Those whom we have just lifted up were helped today by the Body of Christ: each one of you. As you served, no matter what it was that you were asked to do, you did what Jesus did during his time on earth—you cared for those most in need. So let's take the time to celebrate the presence of Christ in you.

4. Invite the participants to stand and form a circle. Select one person to begin, and say the following to the group:

- Turn to the person on your right. Take his or her hands in yours and offer a simple blessing: "May you be blessed for being the hands and feet of Jesus today." (You may wish to refer them to the newsprint should they need to be reminded of the blessing.) Make the sign of the cross on the person's hands. Then invite that person to give the same blessing to the person on his or her right, continuing around the circle.

5. Tell participants to leave the retreat with the challenge to continue to be Christ's body for others at home, at school, and at work in serving others. Invite the participants to sing the closing song you have chosen. Thank them for their participation in the retreat, and then launch into the song.

Simplicity or Stuff: Which Will You Choose?

A Lenten Evening Reflection

Overview

This session is designed as a Lenten evening reflection to engage youth in examining their lives in light of the Gospel challenges to pray, fast, and give alms. Using a justice perspective, the facilitator will lead the young people through activities that place their own spending and consumption habits in relationship to what others have and lack. The participants will study the Church's teachings about living a holy, simple life and making choices about their lifestyles as disciples of Jesus.

Outcomes

◆ The participants will become more aware of the gap between their own spending and possessions and what people their age in developing countries have.

◆ The participants will understand the Gospel challenge to pray, fast, and give alms.

◆ The participants will be challenged to live a simpler lifestyle based on compassion for and solidarity with those who do not have what is needed to live a life of dignity.

Background Reading

◆ This session covers pages 219–223 of *The Catholic Faith Handbook for Youth*.

◆ For further exploration, check out paragraph numbers 1434, 1438, 1969, 2447, 2462, and 2558–2865 and part 4 of the *Catechism*.

Core Session:
Simplicity or Stuff:
Which Will You Choose? (140 minutes)

Preparation

- Gather the following items:
  - ❑ sheets of blank paper
  - ❑ pens or pencils
  - ❑ newsprint
  - ❑ markers, enough for each small group
  - ❑ masking tape
  - ❑ colored markers
  - ❑ white board (optional)
  - ❑ colorful self-stick notes, 3-inch-by-3-inch size, one for each participant
  - ❑ *Catholic Youth Bible*s or other Bibles, at least five copies
  - ❑ copies of *Spirit & Song* or another hymnal
  - ❑ an audiocassette player or a CD player, or a live musician
  - ❑ instrumental music or a recorded song on the theme of sharing (optional)
  - ❑ materials for a prayer center, including a *Catholic Youth Bible* or other Bible, a cross, a large candle, matches, a loaf of bread, and any seasonal decorations
- On newsprint, overheads, or a PowerPoint presentation, prepare the statistics from resource 9, "Touring the Globe: Who Has What?"
- Write each of the following three slogans on a separate sheet of newsprint:
  - ○ live simply so others might simply live
  - ○ until everyone has enough, no one should have too much
  - ○ we must give of our substance, not just of our abundance
- On a sheet of newsprint, write the word "SOLIDARITY" at the top. Include the following suggestions under the word, but leave a significant amount of blank space for the participants to write their suggestions:
  - ○ commit to conserving water
  - ○ give up chocolate one day of the week during Lent.
  - ○ give up television, the Internet, or your portable stereo one day of the week during Lent.
- On a second sheet of newsprint, write the word "PRAYER" at the top. Include the following suggestions under the word, but leave lots of white space for the participants:
  - ○ pray for those who go hungry today
  - ○ pray the Lord's Prayer every morning when you wake up and every night when you go to bed
  - ○ pray for the strength to practice self-denial in order to stand with those who go without

- On a third sheet of newsprint, write the word "SHARING" at the top. Include these suggestions on the sheet:
  - pledge to donate one thing on your personal inventory list
  - pledge for every new thing you buy, you will donate something used to the local Saint Vincent de Paul Agency, Catholic Charities, or a shelter
  - give up buying soda from the vending machines during Lent, and donate the money saved to Catholic Relief Services or your favorite charity
- Select songs for the prayer experiences. The music should emphasize openness to God's will in our lives.
- Select a song for the Act activity on the theme of sharing.
- If you are not familiar with the Touring the Globe activity, you may wish to practice with a group of adults so you are comfortable with the process.
- Establish a prayer center in the space you will be using for this session. Cover a small table with a colorful cloth. Arrange a Bible, a cross, a candle, a loaf of bread, and any seasonal decoration you deem appropriate on the table. Put the prayer center where it will be visible during the session, allowing enough space around the table for participants to gather comfortably for prayer.
- Recruit five readers for the opening prayer.
- Recruit a reader to proclaim Matt. 6:2–18.
- Recruit a reader to proclaim Mark 10:17–22.

Welcome (5 minutes)

1. Welcome the participants to the evening reflection. Give a brief overview of what the participants may expect. Provide a way for participants to introduce themselves to one another.

Opening Prayer: Prayer from the Heart (10 minutes)

1. Invite the participants to join in singing the gathering song you have chosen.

2. Offer this opening prayer:

- Loving God, tonight we come together as pilgrims on a journey to Easter. In the true spirit of Lent, we bring to you our needs, our gifts, and our failings, and especially our gratitude for all you have done for us. We ask you to take all these and bless them. Give us open hearts and minds tonight, that we may hear your will for our lives during our Lenten journey and be your faithful disciples. We ask this in the name of your Son, Jesus. Amen.

3. Invite the reader to come forward and proclaim Matt. 6:7–15. Allow a few moments for quiet reflection.

4. Invite the five readers to lead the participants through "A Lord's Prayer Reflection" in *The Catholic Youth Bible,* near Matt. 6:5–15. Invite the young people to answer each set of reflective questions in their hearts as the readers move through the reflection.

5. Conclude the prayer by inviting the participants to join in singing a song which emphasizes doing God's will.

Involve: Personal Inventory, Juan's Story, Reactions (20 minutes)

1. Begin by telling the participants that they are going to take three quick tours. The first is a personal tour of the things they own and things to which they have easy access. The second is a tour of the life of a teenager from Nicaragua. The third is a tour of what people across the globe have and what they possess.

2. Distribute a sheet of paper and a pen or pencil to each participant. Say:

- I will ask twenty questions to help you do an inventory of things you own or to which you have easy access. For every question to which your answer is "Yes," draw the item mentioned on your paper. Do not worry about details; just represent the item in sketch form.
  - Do you have more than three pairs of shoes?
  - Do you have more than ten CDs?
  - Do you have your own bedroom?
  - Do you have more than $5 in your wallet or purse?
  - Do you own a CD player or other sound system?
  - Do you have a computer in your home?
  - Do you have more than two sweaters?
  - Do you have your own car or access to a family car on a regular basis?
  - Do you have your own cell phone?
  - Do you have a computer game or hand-held game of any kind?
  - Do you have sports equipment worth more than $20?
  - Do you have cosmetics worth more than $10?
  - Have you used a soda machine or other vending machine recently?
  - Have you eaten at a restaurant or fast-food place within the past week?
  - Have you thrown away part of a meal within the past week?
  - Have you used plastic cups, paper plates, paper napkins, or other disposable products within the past week?
  - Have you paid for entertainment such as a movie, an athletic event, or a concert within the past week?
  - Do you own more than ten books?
  - Do you usually eat meat three or more times a week?
  - Do you keep the water running the entire time you brush your teeth?

3. Invite participants to sit comfortably for their second tour. Encourage them to close their eyes and focus on what you are about to read. Then slowly read the following:

- My name is Juan. I am from Nicaragua, where my father was a farmer who grew coffee beans for sale on the international market. We never made a lot of money, just enough to get by, because the companies that bought our beans paid us so little. We always managed until recently. We have had severe drought in our country for over two years, and the world market for coffee beans has been failing. We lost our farm, and my father and mother moved into a slum in Managua, hoping to find work in the capital city. But there is not much work. There is only one room to shelter my parents, my five brothers and sisters, and me. We have been very unhappy in Managua. The shack we live in is drafty. There is no privacy, and there is not enough food to feed all of us. The water we use is contaminated by the raw sewage running through the slum. My little sister, Rosa, is sick, and there is no money for a doctor or for medicine. My brother and I decided to try to get to America so we can make money and send it home to our family. We each took a plastic sack and put two T-shirts, a pair of underwear, one pair of jeans, a piece of fruit, and a sandwich in the sack. Then we said goodbye and left our family. We are now in northern Mexico, seeking help in slipping across the border. We have to do it illegally because America won't allow us in. But what choice do we have? There are no jobs for us in our own country, and in America people get rich and live well. Sometimes I wonder what it would be like to go on a date, eat food in a restaurant, drive a car, or have a new pair of shoes. I have dreams, you know. Doesn't everyone who is seventeen?

4. Ask the participants to open their eyes and to look at the papers they drew of their personal things. Then ask:

- What is your reaction to the inventory and the story?
- What did you see, feel, or think as you did the activity?
- What did you see, feel, or think as you listened to the story?
- How do you feel now about what you have in comparison to Juan and his brother?

Some possible answers may include being embarrassed, guilty, indifferent, or angry. Try to get the participants in touch with their own feelings and have them think about how their spending affects the lives of others. Once they have processed their reactions, ask them to post their inventories in a cluster on the wall.

Explore: Touring the Globe: Who Has What?
Group Analysis: The Web (30 minutes)

1. Tell participants that they are now going to look at what people have from a national and global perspective, rather than a personal one. Have them take their final "tour" by viewing statistics about who has what in the world. Display the statistics you have prepared from resource 9, "Touring The Globe: Who Has What?" Give them enough time with each statistic to absorb its significance.

2. After the participants have had a chance to read the statistics, say:
- By creating a web chart, we are going to analyze the "why" behind the reality you have just witnessed. The web will be used to identify the reasons why some people do not have what they need to live with dignity, while others have too much.

Write the phrase "lack of food" in the middle of a sheet of newsprint or white board. Then ask:
- Why is it—with all the resources in the world—that some people don't have enough of one of the most basic material goods in life: food?
- Name some *immediate* causes of why people around the globe experience a lack of food.

As the participants name reasons, write these around the initial phrase. Use a different colored marker for this. Then say:
- Now let us look at each of the direct causes and identify secondary causes, or the causes of the causes we already listed.

For example, if the participants identified greed as a direct cause why some people lack food, a cause of greed might be fear of not having their own food. If the participants named lack of money as a cause of lack of food, one cause of lack of money might be no jobs. Use a different colored marker to write these secondary causes around each of the primary causes.

3. Now say to the participants:
- Let us begin to make connections and relationships among the causes.
- Can you identify any common threads among the causes, a common feature in many of the primary and secondary causes?

As the participants give their answers, draw lines on your chart to illustrate these threads and how they are connected. End by writing the common threads in the corner of your newsprint or white board.

4. Congratulate the participants, and tell them that they have just completed a structural analysis of an issue of injustice! Now you are going to go a little deeper into the common threads. Organize the participants into small groups of five or six, and have them discuss these questions:
- Do you think God has given enough resources to the world to support all its people?

Try This

If possible, go one level further, identifying causes of the secondary causes. Again, use a different colored marker.

- Is there enough to go around? If so, then why do some people not have what they need to live a life of dignity? Why do some people go to bed hungry every night?

Tell the participants to use the insights from the web chart to summarize their answers. After several minutes, invite each group to share its answers to the questions.

Break (15 minutes)

Reflect: Gospel Challenges, Slogans (30 minutes)

1. Say to the participants:
- Now we are going to look at the issue of possessions and want from a faith perspective. Listen to what Jesus has to say to us in the Sermon on the Mount.

Invite the reader to come forward and proclaim Matt. 6:2–18. Allow a few moments of silence.

2. Give a reflection on the Scripture reading:
- We must remember that Lent is a time in which our Church calls us to practice the three disciplines of prayer, fasting, and giving alms.
- Prayer helps us grow closer to God and figure out God's will for our lives. Prayer also gives us the strength to do what God wants and to resist the temptation to go our own way and become self-indulgent.
- Fasting is a discipline that does not make sense in the material world. Commercials are constantly bombarding us with messages to consume more, pamper ourselves, and so on. Can someone name a commercial that encourages consumption?

Gather a few responses from the participants. Then continue with these comments:
- Self-denial helps us to appreciate what we have and to be grateful for God's abundant blessings in our lives. Giving something up voluntarily strengthens our character. It places us in solidarity with those who cannot have what we have because they live in poverty and need. Giving something up to stand with poor and marginalized people is a radical action, one that Jesus does repeatedly in the Gospels.
- Almsgiving means taking care of those in need. This is Jesus' biggest challenge to us. He says that we will be judged by what we do for the least of our brothers and sisters. Sharing what we have, when we have so much and others have so little, is not really all that charitable. It is what we *should* do as disciples of Jesus.

3. Ask participants to regather in their small groups. Give each group a sheet of newsprint and some markers. Assign them this task:

TryThis

Invite three participants to proclaim the three sections of this Gospel passage: Matt. 6:2–4, 6:5–14, and 6:16–18.

Parish and Family
connections

◆ Ask your parish to be a sponsor of the Rice Bowl, a program of Catholic Relief Services *(www. catholicrelief.org)*. Encourage families to participate in solidarity by participating in the CRS Rice Bowl during Lent.

◆ Encourage the participants to go home and complete an inventory of the things they own as a family. Once they have completed the inventory, they can sit and discuss what they can do as a family to live a simpler life. What can they give away to practice almsgiving? What things that cost them money can they give up and donate the money saved to the Rice Bowl or Catholic Charities?

◆ Encourage the participants to talk to their family about spending less money on Easter candy and presents this spring. Brainstorm things they can do with the money saved, like donating money to the Heifer Project. They could have fun choosing which animals they would like to "buy" for a family in a developing country! (To learn more about the Heifer Project or to make a donation visit their Web site at *www.heifer.org,* or call 800-422-0755.)

• Each group is to come up with a slogan or catchy phrase designed to encourage your peers to live the Gospel challenge by practicing one or all of the Lenten disciplines.

You will want to refer to the three sheets of newsprint with slogans that you prepared earlier.

• You may start from scratch, or use a commercial that encourages you to consume and buy and twist it into a slogan that challenges others to share and conserve.

• You will have 20 minutes to brainstorm slogans and to find a creative way to draw or display your slogan on the newsprint.

4. Ask each group to appoint a spokesperson to share its slogan with the entire community. Invite feedback from the other groups. Then have the spokespersons post their slogans on the walls as reminders to the group to live justly.

Act: Challenges to the Participants (15 minutes)

1. Introduce the action step by proclaiming James 2:14–17. Allow a moment for quiet reflection. Then offer the following comments:

• So far this evening we have talked about being disciples, living simpler lives, and caring for those in need. Now it is time to take action—as the Scriptures challenge you to do!

2. Place the three sheets of newsprint with "SOLIDARITY," "PRAYER," and "SHARING" written on them on three different tables (or on the floor if no tables are available). Have several markers next to each sheet of paper.

3. Say to the participants:

• Now you have the opportunity to work with the Holy Spirit on deciding what you need to do this Lent to simplify your lives, share with others, and be persons of prayer.

Refer to the examples already written on the sheets to illustrate possibilities:

• An example of solidarity is conserving water. While your particular region might have plenty of water, many people in the world do not have access to clean water. A person who wanted to stand in solidarity with them might choose to shower this way: turn the water off once you are wet; then shampoo and soap up, and only turn the water back on when you are ready to rinse. When brushing your teeth, don't run the water while brushing.

• An example of prayer would be praying the Lord's Prayer twice a day, meditating on the abundance of daily "bread" you have and praying for those who go hungry.

- An example of sharing is not adding to the amount of things you already have. This means that every time you buy something new, find something in your closet, drawers, or shelves to donate to a worthy cause or a helping agency. You may be acquiring new stuff, but you won't have more stuff!
- As you visit each of the three action possibilities, read the suggestions, and add your own.

To facilitate this process, divide the participants into three groups, and assign each group to one of the three sheets. After a few minutes, rotate them to the next sheet, and invite them to read the suggestions and add their own. Finally, send the groups to the third sheet, and repeat the process.

4. Post the three sheets on the wall, and say:

- Scan the suggestions until you find one that speaks to you. When you make your choice, sit down, close your eyes, and pray for the strength to keep your commitment.

You may wish to play instrumental music or a song that speaks to sharing in the background while the participants make their selections.

5. When all participants have made a choice, call them back to the large group. Encourage them to live the Gospel this Lent by keeping their commitment to the action they chose. Remind them that prayer will be a necessary part of keeping the commitment.

Pray: Love Beyond Love (15 minutes)

1. Call the participants to prayer by asking them to sing together a song asking Jesus to be the bread for their lives. Invite them to listen closely to the words of the song as they offer their commitment to Jesus. Sing the first three verses of "The Summons," or other song you have chosen.

2. Invite the reader to come forward and proclaim Mark 10:17–22. Allow a few moments for quiet reflection. Then say:

- We are challenged to be stronger than the rich young man in the Gospel. We are encouraged to share our possessions with those in need.

3. Distribute a self-stick note and a pen or pencil to each participant, inviting them to write their action on the note. Say:

- As a response to the Gospel reading we just heard, I invite you to place your note over your personal inventory on the wall as a sign of your willingness to live simpler lives and stand in solidarity with the poor.

4. After they post their notes, have them join in a circle in the middle of the room. To close, sing the fourth and final verse of "The Summons," or other song you have chosen.

- Challenge the participants to go home and add prayer to their family life. How can they pray together as a family during Lent?
- If the participants have younger brothers or sisters, visit the Catholic Relief Services Web site (*www.catholicrelief.org*), and click on "Kids Follow Me!" Interactive games and quizzes help children learn more about poverty, hunger, and debt in developing countries. Encourage the young people to guide their younger siblings through some of these activities.

Spirit & Song connections

- "Bread for the World," by Bernadette Farrell
- "Lead Me, Lord," by John D. Becker
- "Now We Remain," by David Haas
- "Open My Eyes," by Jesse Manibusan
- "Somos el Cuerpo de Cristo/We Are the Body of Christ," by Jaime Cortez
- "The Summons," by John L. Bell

Touring the Globe: Who Has What?

Present these statistics on newsprint, on overhead transparencies, or in a PowerPoint presentation.

- U.S. citizens consume five times more than Mexican citizens.
- U.S. citizens consume ten times more than Chinese citizens.
- U.S. citizens consume thirty times more than Indian citizens.
  (From *www.adbusters.org,* accessed July 3, 2003)

- 20 percent of the world's people consume 86 percent of the world's resources.
- The richest 20 percent of the world's population own 87 percent of the world's vehicles.
  (From the UN Development Programme, *www.globalissues.org/Trade Related/Consumption.asp,* accessed July 3, 2003)

- The average person in the United States eats 1.5 times the food needed to survive; 800 million people in the world don't have enough to eat.
- The amount of money that people in the United States spend on makeup is a little more than what it would cost to provide basic education to all the world's children.
- About 1.2 billion people in the world live on less than $1 a day; the U.S. Department of Labor reports that the average annual pay for a U.S. worker was $35,296 in 2000.
  (From Catholic Relief Services, *www.catholicrelief.org/kids,* accessed July 3, 2003)

- One out of every six children in America lives in poverty. (Catholic Campaign for Human Development, *www.usccb.org/cchd/povertyusa/index.htm,* accessed July 3, 2003.)

- The combined Gross National Product (GNP) of the poorest 48 nations in the world is less than the wealth of the THREE richest nations.
- Nearly one billion people entered the 21st century unable to read a book or to sign their name.
- 12 percent of the world's population uses 85 percent of the world's water.
  (From *www.globalissues.org,* accessed July 3, 2003)

Racism: Our Response
A Half-Day or Evening Retreat Experience

12

Overview

Racism is a sin that violates people's human dignity. Our Baptism requires that we protect and honor the human dignity of each person. In *Renewing the Vision,* the United States Conference of Catholic Bishops (USCCB) writes: "Ministry with adolescents needs to counteract prejudice, racism, and discrimination by example, with youth themselves becoming models of fairness and nondiscrimination" (USCCB, *Renewing the Vision,* p. 23).

This retreat experience helps participants investigate the ways they can respond to racism as Catholic Christians. The experience begins with a simulation game designed to illustrate the many issues that surface when we interact with cultures that are unfamiliar to us. Large-group and small-group discussions help the participants to reflect on racism in their own experience and to begin naming some action steps they can take to combat racism. The retreat ends with a prayer service celebrating the diversity of humankind and asking God for the strength to live out commitments to new action.

Outcomes

◆ The participants will explore the dynamics involved in developing stereotypes, which ultimately lead to racism.
◆ The participants will be able to define racism, discrimination, prejudice, stereotype, and institutional racism.
◆ The participants will identify positive action steps they can take to combat racism.

AT A GLANCE

**Core Session:
Racism:
Our Response
(165 minutes)**

◆ Involve:
Making the Space Safe
(10 minutes)
◆ Involve: Multicolored Cultures Simulation Game
(30 minutes)
◆ Explore: Processing the Simulation Game
(30 minutes)
◆ Break
(15 minutes)
◆ Explore:
Defining the Key Terms
(30 minutes)
◆ Reflect: *Brothers and Sisters to Us,* Our Response from Faith
(10 minutes)
◆ Act: Creating a Plan
(20 minutes)
◆ Pray: Sacred Acts to Change the World
(20 minutes)

Core Session: Racism: Our Response (150 minutes)

Preparation

- Gather the following items:
  - ❑ copies of resource 10, "Cultural Assignments," one group cut out for each participant
  - ❑ copies of handout 11, "Definitions," one for each participant
  - ❑ an audiocassette player or CD player
  - ❑ reflective instrumental background music or live musician, if available
  - ❑ newsprint
  - ❑ markers
  - ❑ masking tape
  - ❑ sheets of blank paper, several for each participant
  - ❑ pens or pencils
  - ❑ snacks for each table
  - ❑ an equal number of slips of paper in pink, yellow, blue, and green, one slip for each participant
  - ❑ a *Catholic Youth Bible* or other Bible
  - ❑ copies of *Spirit & Song* or another hymnal
  - ❑ materials for a prayer center, including a cloth, a *Catholic Youth Bible* or other Bible, a cross, a large candle, matches, and any seasonal decorations
- Recruit two readers, one to proclaim Gen. 1:24–27 and the other to proclaim Luke 10:29–37.
- Establish a prayer center in the space you will be using for this retreat. Cover a small table with a colorful cloth. Arrange a *Catholic Youth Bible* or other Bible, a cross, a candle, and any seasonal decoration you deem appropriate on the table. Put the prayer center where it will be visible during the session, allowing enough space around the table for participants to gather comfortably for prayer.
- Select a gathering song and a closing song to reflect the theme of inclusiveness.
- Post on newsprint the following ground rules for the simulation.
  - ○ We are here to learn how to combat racism in a positive manner. To do this, my role is to make sure our time together is good and our gathering place is safe for all to participate freely.
  - ○ You may hear things and learn things that make you a little uncomfortable. That is okay. Remember to be open to the Spirit encouraging you to learn, change, and grow.
  - ○ When you share with the group, you need to speak for yourself and not for anyone else.

- When someone else speaks, each of us needs to listen to him or her. Being a good listener is very important.
- Our focus is on learning together and finding the areas where we each need to grow. This experience should not be used to accuse others (individuals or specific ethnic groups) of racist actions or attitudes.

Involve: Making the Space Safe (10 minutes)

1. Welcome the participants, and give a brief overview of the retreat experience. Introduce the topic by saying:

- Racism is a very sensitive topic, and discussing it can bring up many emotions.
- Because racism can be a volatile subject, we will establish some "ground rules" so that the session stays positive.
- Let's review the ground rules.

Review the ground rules as noted on the newsprint. Be sure to answer or clarify any questions the participants may have. Then continue by asking:

- Does anyone have a suggestion to add to our ground rules?

Allow time for response and discussion if needed. Then proceed by saying:

- If we respect one another and take care of one another during this session, we can all come away with a deeper understanding of how each of us can combat racism in our society and our world.
- Because I am confident that we will all respect one another throughout this session, let us begin our discussion of racism by moving into a simulation experience.

Involve: Multicolored Cultures Simulation Game (30 minutes)

1. To begin the activity, tell the participants that they will be participating in a simulation experience. Say:

- Although you are bound to find parts of this activity humorous—and you are free to laugh—please take this experience seriously. A great deal can be learned from this activity.

2. Give each participant one of the cutouts you have made from resource 10, "Cultural Assignments." To ensure even distribution, hand out a pink slip, a yellow slip, a blue slip, and a green slip in that order, repeating the pattern as many times as necessary. Make sure there are males and females in all four color groups.

3. Assign a different corner (or space) in the room to each of the four color groups. Ask the participants to gather in the space designated for the color they have been assigned. When everyone has gathered with his or her color group, say:

VARIATION:
Small Group

If you have fewer than 16 participants, follow the directions listed here through step 4. Skip step 5 (which asks the group to subdivide into smaller groups). Each of your four culture groups will remain together, and all the participants can gather in one common location. Continue with the instructions at step 6.

- Each of the four colors represents a different culture. Each group's task is to practice its particular cultural ways, using the information provided on the slip of paper you have been given. Each member in the color group should become familiar with the group's "culture."

Allow 10 minutes for the groups to prepare.

4. Instruct the color groups to divide themselves into four smaller subgroups of equal numbers (or as close as they can get). One of the subgroups should stay at its original location, and the other three subgroups should go to the three other color areas. When all the subgroups have moved, there should be four groups, with subgroups from each of the four cultures. While they are doing this, you will want to put out snacks at each location.

5. Ask the participants to mix and mingle over the snacks. Tell them to behave as naturally as they can while acting out their own particular culture. Allow about 10 minutes of interaction.

(This activity is adapted from Lisa-Marie Calderone-Stewart, *Lights for the World*, pp. 92–93.)

Explore: Processing the Simulation Game (30 minutes)

1. Gather the participants together for a general discussion. Ask one participant from each of the four cultures to read the description of his or her culture's typical behavior. Elicit general comments about the experience. To process the simulation experience, ask participants to finish the following sentences:

- During the activity, I felt . . .
- Something that happened to me was . . .
- Something this activity made me think about was . . .

2. Ask each participant to count the number of times he or she felt insulted during the interaction around the snack table. Total the numbers from the individual participants to come up with one number for the whole group. Expect a large number. Then ask each person to count the number of times he or she purposely tried to insult someone or hurt someone's feelings during the interaction. Expect a smaller number. Ask the group to reflect on the differences between the number of times they felt insulted and the number of times the insult was intended.

3. Finish the discussion of this activity with the following questions:

- If attempts at communicating involve so many unintentional insults, what does this say about our need—as people living in a multicultural society—to understand cultures other than our own?
- Can you describe any real-life misunderstandings like those in this simulation game that you have seen happen between persons of different ethnic and cultural backgrounds?

Examples may include: Asian cultures do not look "elders" in the eye, out of respect, but this can be seen as disrespectful in other cultures. Personal space is different between cultures, so a person from one culture can make someone from a different culture uncomfortable by standing too close. When people from India shake their head from side to side, the gesture communicates "yes" within their culture but is seen as a "no" in American culture.

- Because of this experience, what do you think you would do differently in the ways you treat people from different cultures?

Write responses to these discussion questions on a sheet of newsprint.

(This activity is adapted from Lisa-Marie Calderone-Stewart, *Lights for the World,* pp. 92–93.)

4. Offer the following comments as a way to conclude the simulation activity:

- Before we understood the other "cultures" we shared a snack with, we may have been insulted because they acted out of their own cultural values, which were different from our own.
- Often we form judgments about the actions of people from a different culture without fully understanding their culture or their values.
- These judgments eventually become generalizations that we use to describe all people from that culture.
- When enough people believe these generalizations, they become stereotypes that become a "belief" of a culture. For example, we probably all know some very smart people. However, if someone is blonde, he or she fights against a stereotype that blonde people are dumb. We may know this to be a "joke," but often it becomes a hurdle for blondes (especially females) to overcome. This is just one example that is not based on culture or race. I am sure that you can think of stereotypes based on race and culture.
- Stereotypes are very dangerous because they take away our need to understand people who are different from us. We do not take the time to understand people when we already have them categorized in our minds.

Break (15 minutes)

Explore: Defining the Key Terms (30 minutes)

1. Gather the participants into a large group. Introduce the next part of the retreat in this way:

- We have had an opportunity to simulate on a small scale some of the dynamics involved in forming stereotypes. Now it is important to define some of the words we are using so that the discussion becomes clearer.

VARIATION:
Gender Groups
Separate the boys and the girls, and ask them to create a list of the top ten gender stereotypes they most often deal with. Compare the two lists.

2. Distribute a copy of handout 11, "Definitions," to all participants and review it with them. Be sure to clarify any questions they might have.

3. Organize the participants into small groups of eight, or use the culture groups from the previous activity if your numbers are small. Say:
- Look at the five definitions on the handout, and find examples of these definitions in your own lives, in your communities, in the world.

Allow 15 minutes for this activity.

4. Have the small groups re-gather and report on their examples of each definition. Allow time for discussion. Use these discussion questions:
- Was it difficult to think of examples? How so?
- If it wasn't difficult, what does that say about our society?
- If it was difficult, did hearing other people's reports trigger any ideas?
- What are you challenged to do?

Reflect: *Brothers and Sisters to Us,* Our Response from Faith (10 minutes)

1. Introduce this process as an opportunity to get to know a pastoral letter written by our U.S. bishops. Include the following points:
- *Brothers and Sisters to Us: U.S. Bishops' Pastoral Letter on Racism in Our Day* is a document that addresses what we believe about racism and challenges us to respond to the problem of racism as disciples of Christ.
- The document defines racism as "the sin that says some human beings are inherently superior and others essentially inferior because of race. It is the sin that makes racial characteristics the determining factor for the exercise of human rights."
- Racism is a sin that discriminates against people because of the color of their skin.
- Racism is a sin because it denies human beings their dignity, a dignity that comes from God.
- Because racism is a sin and because it denies people their human dignity, we must do something to change the situation.
- The bishops write:

  "Racism is not merely one sin among many; it is a radical evil that divides the human family and denies the new creation of a redeemed world. To struggle against it demands an equally radical transformation in our own minds and hearts as well as in the structure of our society."

Action: Creating a Plan (20 minutes)

1. In group discussion, review the experiences participants have had throughout this retreat. Then say:

- Now you are going to have the opportunity to discern what you can do to initiate some "holy change" in your own lives and in your own communities. Enough holy changes can lead to some radical change in the world.

2. Distribute paper and pens, and give the participants some time by themselves to reflect on the day's events and to write one or two action steps to which they are going to commit in order to combat racism. For example, they could commit themselves never to participate in racist jokes. Or they could resolve to experience the gifts of another culture by attending liturgy in an ethnically diverse parish or by going to an ethnic restaurant. They could resolve to meet people of other cultures and be open to the possibility of a friendship when they do.

3. Play some quiet, reflective music in the background while they do this. After 10 minutes, gather the participants together, and let them know they will have an opportunity to pray one of these action steps aloud during the prayer service.

Pray: Sacred Acts to Change the World (20 minutes)

1. Prepare the participants for the closing prayer by telling them that you will begin with a song, followed by an opening prayer. They will then hear the Word proclaimed, after which, as a sign of solidarity against racism, they will be invited to pray aloud their action steps so that you all can pray for one another. Tell them that together we can combat racism in our homes, our communities, and our world, and that we will conclude the prayer with the sign of peace and a song to celebrate our commitment.

2. Gather everyone together in a circle around the prayer table, and invite the participants to join in singing the gathering song you have chosen.

3. Share the following opening prayer:
- Glory to you, God of justice and peace, for sending Jesus the Christ, who teaches us how to live peacefully and walk justly. In him, we know the ultimate victory of justice over injustice, and peace over war. All praise and honor be yours through Christ and the Holy Spirit forever and ever. Amen.

(Edward F. Gabriele, *Prayers for Dawn and Dusk*, p. 185.)

4. Invite the first reader to come forward and proclaim Gen. 1:24–27. Allow a few moments for quiet reflection. Then say:
- We are all male and female, black and white and yellow and brown, created in God's image. Because of this, we are all called to be holy; we are called to be loving creatures made in the very image of our Creator.

5. Invite the second reader to proclaim Luke 10:29–37. Allow a few moments for quiet reflection. Then say:

• These prophetic words still ring true for us today: "Go and do likewise."

6. Invite those who feel comfortable doing so to share aloud their action steps.

• Our response to each statement is, "With God, I will have the strength."

7. While still in a circle, begin a sign of peace in this way:

• Have a designated leader place his or her hands over the hands of the person on the left and say, "Peace be with you." Invite the person to respond, "And also with you." That person should then turn to the person on his or her left and repeat the sign of peace. This ritual should progress completely around the circle until it returns to the designated leader.

8. Invite the participants to join in singing the closing song you have selected.

9. Conclude the prayer by saying:

• May the peace we share with one another today extend to all the peoples of the world. We ask you, God, to give us the courage and the wisdom that we need to live peaceful lives and to combat racism in our daily choices and interactions. May we follow the example of Jesus and treat each person with dignity. We ask this through Christ, our Lord. Amen.

Cultural Assignments

Pink Group
- You are very affectionate and hang out in groups of two or more.
- You always greet with a hug—even when greeting a stranger.
- You are insulted and feel rejected whenever someone sees you and doesn't hug you.
- You like to talk about your family.
- You steer all conversation back to the topic of family.
- You love to eat and share with others.

Yellow Group
- You are loners and travel alone.
- You don't touch anyone except members of your immediate family, and that is never done in public.
- You are insulted and feel violated if someone touches you in public.
- You try to stay a full arm's length away from others.
- You like to talk about current events from the news.
- You steer all conversation back to news items.
- You love to eat and believe it is a very spiritual experience that a person should do alone.

Blue Group
- You believe men are superior to women.
- Males in your culture call all females "girl."
- Females call all males "sir."
- Females obey males and always try to please them.
- Males are insulted if females do not show them signs of submission.
- Females are frightened of males who treat them as equals.
- You like to talk about animals, especially if you are a male.

Green Group
- You believe women are superior to men.
- Females in your culture call all males "boy."
- Males call all females "ma'am."
- Males obey females and always try to please them.
- Females are insulted if males do not show them signs of submission.
- Males are frightened of females who treat them as equals.
- You love to talk about flowers, trees, and other plants, especially if you are a female.

(This resource is adapted from *Lights for the World: Training Youth Leaders for Peer Ministry,* by Lisa-Marie Calderone-Stewart [Winona, MN: Saint Mary's Press, 1995], handout 4–A. Copyright © 1995 by Saint Mary's Press. All rights reserved.)

Definitions

- **Discrimination:** the act or intention of making prejudicial generalizations about another race in order to accuse or devalue a person of a different race. Discrimination directly influences a person's ability to access services or make a living.

- **Prejudice:** a body of unfounded opinions or attitudes about an individual, or group, that represents them in an unfavorable light.

- **Stereotype:** a generalized set of traits and characteristics attributed to a specific ethnic, national, cultural, or racial group which gives rise to false expectations that individual members of the group will conform to these traits.

- **Racism:** the sin that says some human beings are inherently superior and others essentially inferior because of race. It is a sin to make racial characteristics the determining factor for the exercise of human rights.

- **Institutional (or systemic) racism:** when institutions—governments, legal, medical, and educational systems, and businesses—discriminate against certain groups of people based on race, color, ethnicity, or national origin. Often unintentional, such racism occurs when the apparently non-discriminatory actions of the dominant culture have the effect of excluding or marginalizing minority cultures.

(The definition of *racism* on this handout is from *Brothers and Sisters to Us: U.S. Bishops' Pastoral Letter on Racism in Our Day* [1979], by the United States Conference of Catholic Bishops, at *www.osjspm.org/cst/racism.htm,* accessed July 18, 2003. Used with permission.

The remaining definitions on this handout are adapted from information on the Racism. No Way! Web site, *www.racismnoway.com.au,* accessed July 7, 2003.)

Part D

Strategies for Justice and Service Work with Youth

Planning Effective Service Projects with Youth

Overview

Service is an essential component of discipleship and can be life-changing for young people. It connects them in a face-to-face way with those who are in need, gives them the opportunity to share their gifts and talents, and encourages them to work for justice for all of God's people. Good service projects do not just happen—they require careful planning, implementation, and follow-up. The following tips for conducting service projects with youth are based on the real-life experiences and wisdom of youth ministers from across the country.

Getting Started

If you are new to service projects with youth, start simply. Connect with an existing service agency (Habitat for Humanity, for example) that handles all the logistics at the work site. You will then be free to focus on preparing the youth for the experience and reflecting on it with them after the event. Leave the technicalities to the experts!

Work *with*, Not for

Whenever possible, have the youth work *with,* not just for, the victims of injustice whom they are serving. It is important that the young people see the poor as people with gifts and talents to share and that they see empowerment and dignity as more important than a handout. Service with young people should have a human face. If you are doing a fund-raiser for a serving organization, find a way to have the youth deliver the raised funds to the service site, experience a tour of the agency, and talk to the people being served. If the work you are doing is to benefit an international agency, ask for pictures and biographical sketches of some of the people being served so that you can share them with the young people.

Variety Can Be Key

With younger teens, go for breadth in service projects. Expose them to many different types of service experiences, from painting the fence of a disabled person to visiting the elderly, from donating time at a local food pantry, or tutoring young children at the Boys and Girls Club. As youth acquire more experience, shift them from breadth to depth. Invite the older youth to choose service that matches the talents and gifts God has given them. Encourage them to commit to a particular service for a semester or a year. With younger teens, choose a service project that allows them to see the results of their efforts (such as picking up garbage in a vacant lot or bagging food at a food pantry). Move them into more relational services as they mature in their service experience (serving as mentors for central-city children, for example). Once the youth have had significant service experience, encourage them to become advocates for change (advocating with the legislature to get the minimum wage raised, for example).

Prepare, Prepare, Prepare

Prepare the young people for the service experience. Talk to them about what they will hear and see and smell when they arrive on the service site. Equip them with tools for success (for example, if they are going to a nursing home, tell them what older people enjoy discussing). Ensure that they have realistic expectations and that they do not go in thinking they will save the world. Challenge them to be open to the experience and to whatever they are asked to do on-site. Remind them that they are there to help others and that the task they are given is the one most needed, even if it is not the type of work they were hoping to do. Prepare adult chaperones for the service experience. Do you want them to hold back and let the youth find their own way through the experience? Do you want the adults to model the service you are asking the young people to do? It is important that chaperones understand their role in the service experience.

Flexibility

Be flexible, and always have a "Plan B." For example, if you plan a service experience outdoors and it rains, what is your backup plan? If an agency is counting on you to bring fifteen youth to reorganize the food pantry and only five youth show up, what will you do? Living up to a commitment to a helping agency should be a top priority for any service project.

Reflect, Reflect, Reflect

Always engage youth in theological reflection following a service experience. This can be as simple as discussing their service while driving back to the parish or school, giving them a journal sheet to take home with them, or processing the experience over pizza. A separate gathering for reflection is not necessary. Your goal is to put the experience of service in dialogue with the faith of the young people. Appropriate questions may include: What happened to your heart today? How were you the Body of Christ for the people you served? How were *they* the Body of Christ for you? Where did you see sin today? Where did you see grace? Include an appropriate Scripture passage, or quote from Catholic social teaching to tie the experience together at the end of the process.

Celebrate

Find ways to celebrate the service of young people. Be an advocate for youth by letting the whole parish know the good work they are doing. This could be through a bulletin announcement, praying for the youth at Sunday liturgy, or having the young people share their service experience with the congregation before or after Sunday liturgy.

Service Involvement, Not Service Hours

Emphasize service, not number of hours, when doing a service project with young people. When you scrupulously count hours, youth will focus on the quantity of their service rather than the purpose of serving. Letting them choose their service from a list of possibilities you give them will give them ownership of their work and encourage them to continue choosing service as a natural part of life rather than as a requirement for being confirmed.

Involve Families

Involve the families of young people in service work. Teenagers are more likely to embrace service as a lifelong practice if they experience it with their parents and siblings. In addition, serving as families strengthens the family bond, gives families quality time together, and provides an opportunity for shared reflection after the service experience. Agencies appreciate family participation as well, and the intergenerational approach is enriching for agency clients as well as for the families.

Selecting Appropriate Service Sites

It is important to remember that the purpose of a service project is helping those in need. When doing service as a part of youth ministry, it is equally important that the service puts into action what young people are learning about their Christian responsibility to be people of justice. A good service agency provides an experience of service that puts young people face to face with a particular need of the community. When choosing an appropriate service agency, keep the following criteria in mind:

Have a reliable contact with whom to make all necessary arrangements. This will often be a volunteer coordinator, someone whose primary responsibility is working with volunteers. A reliable contact can make the difference between a service project that is successful and one that requires a "Plan B"! Be sure to clarify with your contact the specific work the young people will be doing. Communicate to the coordinator the age and size of the group so that the service is age appropriate.

Make contact with the service agency more than once. If the service site is not one that frequently has youth volunteers, talk to the volunteer coordinator about working with the youth from your parish, their experience of service, and their abilities. Ask the volunteer coordinator to give the young people an orientation so they know why clients need the agency, what the agency does to help others, and the purpose behind the work which the young people will be doing. Suggest that the orientation be short and to the point for the youth will be eager to get to the actual work of the day.

Choose an agency that is youth-friendly. Many agencies work regularly with youth volunteers; others do not. If the agency you are considering has little experience with young people, make sure it is a place that *values* young people. If not, it can be a bad experience for youth and a burden on the agency. A good way to check on this is to ask the agency to provide you with the names of other youth ministers who have brought young people to volunteer there. These youth ministers will be a good source of information on how youth-responsive the agency really is. Choose an agency that can use the help the young people desire to give. There are few things more disappointing than arriving at a service agency only to discover that it did not really need your help.

Be sure that the working conditions are safe. A good service agency will have measures in place to ensure the safety of volunteers. It is important not to assume, so ask questions. For example, if you will be working to rehabilitate houses for low-income families, make sure that the young people are given the proper safety equipment. Know in advance whether the group might be split up into smaller groups. If so, bring enough adults to accommodate the situation.

Choose a service agency that will expose young people to the real needs and issues surrounding the service they will be doing. A good orientation to the service agency is a great way to help young people see how the service they will be doing contributes to the overall mission of the agency. Having an opportunity to meet or work with people who are being served by the agency is another great way for young people to learn more about the causes and consequences of real need.

14 Researching Justice Issues

Overview

Abundant resources exist for pursuing information about issues of social justice. Church resources, the Internet and mass media, local and national organizations, and individuals in your own area can all be helpful in providing what you need to become knowledgeable about a subject. If you or the young people are passionate about or interested in an issue for which you do not have a pre-planned session, here are some strategies for getting started, learning more, making connections, and reaching out. The issue of immigration will be used to illustrate the research possibilities.

Getting Started

A good place to start investigating an issue for faith-based action or information is by asking the question, "What does the Church say?" Church documents speak to numerous issues of social justice. Several collections of Catholic social teaching documents have been published; many of them include commentaries on implementation.

- *Catholic Social Teaching: Our Best Kept Secret,* by Peter J. Henriot, Edward P. DeBerri, and Michael J. Schultheis (Maryknoll, NY: Orbis Books and the Center for Concern, Washington, 1992, third revised and enlarged edition) is a short, easy-to-use index of documents and statements written between 1891 and 1991. It offers a breakdown of the major papal letters and several statements by national conferences of bishops. In the breakdown of *Populorum Progressio* in *Our Best Kept Secret,* one section refers to the topic of "welcoming others . . . especially migrant workers." Finding the referenced document can give some insight into a papal view of the treatment of immigrants.

- *A Concise Guide to Catholic Social Teaching,* by Kevin E. McKenna (Notre Dame, IN: Ave Maria Press, 2002) references social documents under the heading of the seven principles of Catholic social teaching.

- Full texts of many papal documents can be found online at the Web site of the Office of Social Justice for the Archdiocese of Saint Paul and Minneapolis, *www.osjspm.org.*
- A visit to the United States Conference of Catholic Bishops (USCCB) Web site is an excellent way to find the most recent statements on an issue. Go to *www.usccb.org,* and select "Statements," "Subject Listing" and then click on "International Policy," "Migration," or "Social Justice." Another USCCB option is to select "Departments" on the home page, and select the department of "Migration and Refugee Services" and the department of "Social Development and World Peace." Both departments provide resource for dioceses, parishes, and individual Catholics who are interested in information and action on issues of social justice.
- To further your knowledge of Church teaching on a justice issue, refer to the table of contents and the index of the *Catechism of the Catholic Church.* Although the *Catechism* does not directly address all justice issues, broader topics such as social justice, solidarity, poverty, and the common good are discussed. A *Catechism* paragraph you find helpful may also have references of its own that lead to other documents or to Scripture passages.
- An almost indispensable publication is the *Scripture Guide,* published by the Catholic Campaign for Human Development (Washington, DC: USCCB, 1998). This eight-page resource lists social justice references in the Bible, grouped by the themes of Catholic social teaching. The booklet can be ordered through the Publishing Office of the USCCB (800-235-8722). The publication number is 5-229 (English) or 5-230 (Spanish).

Learning More

After discovering the Church's view and history on an issue of justice (continuing to use immigration as our example), it is time to learn more about the topic locally, nationally, and even internationally. There are many media formats from which to choose.

- Start with a local or national newspaper (your local paper, *USA Today,* or your diocesan paper).
- Search the Internet (use your favorite search engine to search for "U.S. immigration policy" or "U.S. border issues immigration" or similar keywords for your designated justice topic).
- Read both secular and Catholic magazines *(Time, Newsweek, America)* for information about your issue.
- Television news and the radio can be more hit-and-miss, but tuning in regularly to local and national news, CNN, or National Public Radio will keep you up-to-date on current government immigration policy and public opinion, as well as many other justice issues.

Making Contact

When you have familiarized yourself with the issue, contact organizations that can teach you more and bring an issue to life.

- Call your diocesan social justice office to get information on current or past initiatives that are relevant to the chosen topic. If the office is not working on your issue, ask whether they know who is addressing the issue.
- Check with Catholic Charities to see whether this agency provides services for immigrants, migrant workers, or refugees in your area. You can also contact other service agencies in your area that address the topic you are researching.
- Call your state Catholic Conference to find out whether it is tracking any related bills or initiatives in the state legislature. This office may have information on particular legislation that is pending in your state and is trained to teach you how to lobby your representatives for a change that the Church supports. To locate your state's director, go to the Web site of the National Association of State Catholic Conference Directors *(www.nasccd.org)*.
- Make contact with the nearest Legal Aid office, which can be a good resource for finding out who else in the community is working with immigrant populations as well as other justice issues.
- Contact other nonprofit organizations. New immigrants are often in need of housing, medical care, food, and other necessities. Organizations that provide these services have information about recent trends and the plight of newly arrived immigrants.

Reaching Out

After learning about a justice topic, you will naturally want to do something to make a difference. By the time you have done all the research, you will probably have many ideas for taking action. Ideas for reaching out include:

Direct Service

- Work to help people who are in immediate need by providing goods or labor.
- Collect food, clothing, or other items that immigrants in your area can use. Find out what is most needed and what is not needed before you begin.
- Volunteer to teach classes in English as a second language (ESL).
- Provide child care for working parents.
- Offer a summer Vacation Bible School in an area that may not otherwise have one.
- Volunteer at an agency that serves an immigrant population.
- Adopt a family at Christmas.
- As a parish, commit to hosting a refugee family from another country.

Learn More

- Invite someone who works with immigrants on a regular basis to speak to the group or parish as a whole.
- Invite an immigrant to speak to the group or parish about the experience of coming to live in the United States.

Speak Out

- Join in local initiatives to protect immigrant rights.
- Follow the issue in your state legislature by keeping in touch with your state Catholic Conference or by searching your state government's Web site. Write to your representatives, telling them what you have learned about immigrants in your area and what action you think the state should take on their behalf.
- Follow national developments on the issue by visiting the United States Conference of Catholic Bishops Web site regularly at *www.usccb.org* and the Web sites of Congress at *www.senate.gov* and *www.house.gov*. Write to your senators and representatives about your views on how immigrants should be treated in our country.

Other Web Resources

- Catholic Relief Services at *www.catholicrelief.org*
  - CRS educates the people of the United States to fulfill their moral responsibilities toward our brothers and sisters around the world by helping the poor, working to remove the causes of poverty, and promoting social justice. In addition, CRS provides direct aid and offers opportunities to be involved in the development and realization of the potential of those in poverty.
- Center of Concern at *www.coc.org*
  - COC offers moral vision and provides effective leadership in the struggle to end hunger, poverty, environmental decline, and injustice in the United States and around the world. The organization provides reliable information and analysis on development issues, practical alternatives to current development policies, practical suggestions for personal action, and faith reflections on this work for justice.
- Church World Service at *www.churchworldservice.org*
  - CWS assists communities in responding to disasters, resettles refugees, promotes fair national and international policies, and provides educational resources. CWS also offers opportunities to join a people-to-people network of local and global caring through participation in programs such as Crop Walk, Tools of Hope, and Gift of the Heart Kit.

- NETWORK, A National Catholic Social Justice Lobby, at *www.network lobby.org*
  - ○ NETWORK supports and builds political will to develop a just, participatory, and sustainable world community. Founded as a contemporary response to the ministry of Jesus, NETWORK uses Catholic social teaching and the life experience of people who are poor as lenses for viewing social reality.
- Salt of the Earth at *salt.claretianpubs.org*
  - ○ *Salt* is an online resource for social justice. On this Web site you will find articles, strategies and ideas, a chat room, and a message board, all focused on social justice issues.
- Catholic Campaign for Human Development at *www.usccb.org/cchd/index.htm*
  - ○ CCHD is the domestic anti-poverty, social justice program of the U.S. Catholic bishops. Its mission is to address the root causes of poverty in the United States through promotion and support of community-controlled, self-help organizations and through transformative education.
- United Nations High Commission for Human Rights at *www.unhchr.ch*
  - ○ The mission of the Office of the United Nations High Commissioner for Human Rights (OHCHR) is to protect and promote human rights for all people.
- World Factbook at *www.odci.gov/cia/publications/factbook/index.html*
  - ○ The Central Intelligence Agency Directorate of Intelligence produces The World Factbook, a comprehensive resource of facts and statistics on more than 250 countries and other entities.

Doing Advocacy with Youth

15

Overview

The Catholic Church recognizes two basic ways of doing justice, often called the two feet of Christian service. One "foot" is the direct act of charity offered to alleviate the suffering of others. The second foot is championing the rights of poor, voiceless, and marginalized people. Teaching young people how to advocate for others is an important element of ministry. The following are suggestions for advocacy you can add to your direct service programs or do independently with youth.

Choose an Issue

A good way to choose a national issue is to log on to the Web site for NET-WORK, A National Catholic Social Justice Lobby *(www.networklobby.org)*. At the Web site, click on "Legislative Issues," then on "Priority Issues" for the current year. This site analyzes the bills coming before the House of Representatives and the Senate in the current legislative session and selects several key issues about which people of faith should take a stand. Over the years, NETWORK's priorities have included such topics as welfare reform, housing, global peace, and campaign finance reform.

Get the Facts

Use the ideas for researching justice issues in the previous chapter of this manual to get information on justice issues. It is critical to have accurate information before writing a letter, boycotting a product, or taking any action to stand with the vulnerable. A rumor that a fast-food restaurant supports abortion is not a valid reason to boycott the restaurant. Go to the source to make sure you have the right information.

National Issues

Encourage youth to analyze who has the power to make changes to improve the lives of those for whom they are advocating. In some cases, it is government. The challenge here is to decide which branch of government—legislative, judicial, or executive—is in a position to do something to make the change happen. For example, it may not be strategic to advocate with your member of Congress to vote pro-life if there is currently no bill before Congress on the issue. When true change can only come through the Supreme Court's overturning *Roe v. Wade,* you need to focus on the appointment of new justices. Because the President chooses Supreme Court nominees, it would be appropriate to advocate with the executive branch of government for the nomination of judges who have a pro-life stance. The White House comment line is 202-456-1111, and the e-mail address is *president@white house.gov.*

When a bill is before the Senate or the House of Representatives, provide the young people with the tools to contact their representatives. They can log on to the U.S. Senate at *www.senate.gov* and to the House of Representatives at *www.house.gov.* The Library of Congress Web site identifies current bills, lists the members of Congress who are on the committees dealing with those bills, and tracks how individual Senators and Representatives vote on the bills. The Library of Congress Web site is at *thomas.loc.gov.* Because so much happens in committee on Capitol Hill, it may sometimes be more effective to lobby with the committee chair or committee members than with your own representative if he or she is not on that particular committee.

An independent Web site that also tracks congressional issues and votes is *www.vote-smart.org.* This site has a section devoted to young voters and may be particularly helpful in preparing high school seniors for their first voting experience. Other Web sites with information on policy and issues include The Urban Institute *(www.urban.org)* and the General Accounting Office *(www.gao.gov).*

Research shows that e-mail messages and phone calls do make a difference to elected officials. Legislative assistants tally these messages and pass on constituents' comments to the senators and representatives.

State Issues

For state issues, check with your state Catholic Conference. If you do not know your Catholic Conference representative, go to the Web site of the National Association of State Catholic Conferences *(www.nasccd.org).* Names, addresses, phone numbers, and e-mail addresses are listed for each state's Catholic Conference representative.

Advocating with Faith

For tips on how to lobby from a faith perspective, go to the Web site of NETWORK, A National Catholic Social Justice Lobby *(www.network lobby.org)*. NETWORK provides suggestions for writing letters and for visiting legislators. NETWORK also provides specific ways to influence elected officials at every stage in the legislative process. Click on "What You Can Do" to obtain that information.

Hunger Relief

An organization with concrete suggestions for advocating specifically for hunger relief is Bread for the World. Its Web site, *www.bread.org,* has a "Write to Congress" and a "How to Help" section with recommendations for advocating for the world's hungry and starving people.

Amnesty International

Amnesty International *(www.amnesty.org)* advocates for the release of those unjustly imprisoned. It has numerous chapters across the globe, many of which include youth.

Economic Advocacy

In some cases, those with the power to make a difference are the people who have economic means (the media, corporations, and wealthy people, for example). Companies and corporations that pay unjust wages, practice discrimination, do not promote women, are subsidiaries of larger corporations which deal with arms or tobacco, or practice other forms of injustice pay attention to advocates when their profits are threatened. It is important to teach teenagers that they have power to effect change by the choices they make in spending their money. Supporting companies that practice justice and boycotting those that do not are advocacy stances that can make a difference.

Public Witness

Advocacy can be done effectively through public witness. Young people can participate in a public prayer service (for instance, a justice-oriented stations of the cross done in a downtown area on Good Friday or a prayer chain for life on January 22) to advocate for a faithful position on a current issue. The Catholic Campaign for Human Development *(www.usccb.org/cchd)* has prayer resources with a justice focus to help you prepare your own service. Examples include the *Novena for Justice and Peace* (no. 5-237), *A Justice Prayer Book* (No. 5-231), and *A Scriptural Rosary for Justice and Peace* (no.5-234).

Using the Scriptures to Educate Youth

Overview

Justice and service with young people should always be grounded in the Scriptures, both the Old and the New Testament. The Scriptures help them understand that the discipleship to which Jesus calls them challenges them to care for "the least of their brothers and sisters" (Matt., ch. 25).

The following strategies can put youth in contact with the Word through a justice lens.

Dialogue About Biblical Connections to Justice Issues

Engage young people in dialogue with the Word so that it comes alive for them. Use creative means to proclaim the Word.

- Consider rewriting a passage of the Scripture in a contemporary setting or writing a sequel. What happens after the Scripture writer concluded?
- Invite young people to be eyewitnesses to the Scripture passage being proclaimed.
- Engage all the senses as young people listen to the Word.
- Invite young people to act out a particular passage.
- Use music to illustrate a passage. Many good contemporary liturgical songs have lyrics straight from the Scriptures.
- Show a film of a Scripture story.
- Provide journal questions for the young people to ponder individually and reflectively.
- Use *lectio divina* to break open a Scripture passage. Chapter 34 of *The Catholic Faith Handbook for Youth* includes a discussion on this method of prayer.
- Have young people conduct a Scripture search by giving them a justice theme and then challenging them to find biblical passages illustrating that theme.

Connecting to Catholic Social Teaching

Make connections between the seven principles of Catholic social teaching and the Word. Demonstrate that the source of the principles is the Word of God. Examples include:

- life and dignity of the human person (Gen. 1:27)
- community and the common good (Acts 4:32–35)
- rights and responsibilities (Gal. 6:2)
- option for the poor (Deut. 24:17–22)
- dignity of work (Luke 3:10–18)
- solidarity (Matt. 25:31–46)
- care for God's creation (Gen. 2:15)

Scripture Resources

Take advantage of available resources to help young people understand the meaning of a particular justice passage in the Scriptures.

- *The Catholic Youth Bible* has dynamic ways of focusing on selected Scripture passages throughout the Old and the New Testament. Examples of articles focusing particularly on justice include the following:
  - "Jesus and Civil Disobedience," near Matt. 21:12–13
  - "If You Want Peace, Work for Justice," near Isa. 58:6–14
  - "The Greed Trap," near Luke 12:13–21
  - "The Favorite," near James 2:1–13
- Many *Youth Updates* from St. Anthony Messenger Press *(www.american catholic.org)* focus on justice and make solid scriptural connections. Examples include:
  - "Happy Hunger: Revisiting the Sermon on the Mount" (Y1291)
  - "Wrestling with the Death Penalty" (Y0696)
  - "Protecting God's Creation" (Y0799)
  - "Keeping the Peace: Attitudes and Approaches" (Y0397)
- *Scripture from Scratch—A Popular Guide to Understanding the Bible,* also from St. Anthony Messenger Press, is a great resource for the adult leader to prepare for sharing Scripture passages with youth. Examples of justice-focused issues include:
  - "Do We Love Our Enemies? The Bible and the Just War Tradition" (N0996)
  - "When the Prophets Roared for Justice" (N0298)
  - "Outside the Camp? Leprosy, AIDS, and the Bible" (N1098)
  - "Jesus' 'Plain' Sermon on the Mount" (N0199)
- A good Scripture commentary or concordance provides accurate insights into Scripture passages related to justice.

Preparing Speakers and Panel Members

Overview

Inviting members of the parish and local community to serve as program or event speakers offers the opportunity to incorporate an intergenerational approach to the youth ministry program. The young people benefit from the knowledge, experience, and expertise of local community members. Consider the following suggestions for making the most of speakers and panels in your program efforts.

Professionals Versus Volunteers

Accessing professionals who work full-time with social or justice issues has definite benefits. In addition to the knowledge and experience they bring, they bear witness to the ways people combine their talents, gifts, and compassion for those in need into full-time employment or ministry. Some are called to give their whole energy to issues of justice and service.

Volunteers, for their part, provide benefits of their own. Most often, young people will end up employed outside the social service sector. Their jobs probably will not connect directly with issues of justice and service. Yet they can still share their gifts and energy with those in need through regular volunteering. Presentations from potential role models who give of themselves outside their "day job" can be inspiring to the young people.

Local Speakers

In some ways, the more local a speaker is, the more effective she or he can be long-term. Hearing an effective speaker can be a great learning experience—but the lesson and learnings are reinforced if young people run into the speaker on a regular basis at parish or school events or at the local supermarket. Using local speakers also strengthens the possibility of ongoing involvement with them—as regular speakers, service leaders, or justice mentors for interested youth.

Comfort with Youth

Look for people who genuinely like being around and talking with youth, do not talk down or patronize young people, and are comfortable working with young volunteers.

Offering the Facts and the Feel of an Issue

Those who work regularly with people in need can be a storehouse of information about the causes and consequences of various justice issues. Knowing the facts and the realities of a situation serves as a great springboard for conscious action. However, young people, like most adults, also need to have a "feel" for the issue. They need to know the stories behind the facts and have a sense of the real-life consequences of need and injustice on people such as themselves.

Prepare for Success

Careful and conscientious preparation enhances the likelihood of success. Be clear about your expectations of presenters, and give them plenty of time to prepare for the event. Meet with each speaker prior to the event. Tell him or her about the young people of your parish and their involvement with justice and service activities. Be clear about the program and the role you would like the speaker to play. Share the experiences, questions, and concerns the young people will bring to the dialogue. Answer any questions the speaker has about the group, the program, or the presentation.

Be Clear on the Details

Make sure presenters are clear on the time, length, and focus of their presentation. No matter how good a presenter is, too long is still too long—especially when the speaker is one of several panelists. Emphasize the balance needed between supplying the facts of the issue and telling the real-life stories behind the statistics. Invite an informal and personal approach. Encourage speakers to include personal comments or anecdotes that help participants see how important the issue and people affected are to them personally. Make sure you and the speakers are in agreement about taking questions from the group.

Consider providing each speaker with a copy of handout 12, "Preparing a Justice Presentation."

Communicate Fully and Regularly

Put everything in writing. Follow up your preparation meeting with speakers with a reminder call, card, or e-mail. Be sure you and/or the participants send a thank-you card or note after the event.

Preparing a Justice Presentation

The following questions are meant to help you focus your presentation. They include the particular elements that you need addressed.

- Describe the work that you do.

- Why did you get involved in this work? What motivated you?

- What is the purpose of your agency/service provider? What are the actual services offered?

- Why was your agency established? What economic conditions, cultural issues, and history led to the need for your agency?

- Can you share illustrations or stories of people who seek out your services? What is their history? Why do they come to you? What are their hopes for the future?

- What good does your work accomplish? Do you think you make a difference?

- What keeps you going?

- How can young people support the good work of your agency through direct aid and advocacy for your clients?

18 Learning from Other Cultures

Overview

God is alive and active—in history, in people, and in the history of people. As we grow in appreciation of the giftedness of diverse cultures, we come to know God better as the source of all gifts. This can be especially true as we encounter cultures (racial, ethnic, linguistic, and religious) that are different from our own or are sometimes viewed as "poor" because of their financial needs. For people of faith, dignity (individual and communal) is bestowed not by economic status but by God's creative love. Exploring other cultures by listening to their songs and stories, celebrating their history and holidays, and meeting, eating, and praying with them can be a doorway to true solidarity, in which we recognize our oneness in the Lord and commit ourselves to work together for the common good. Consider the following approaches to helping the young people explore the richness of your community's cultural heritages and traditions.

Start with the Family

better understanding of justice

History

Invite the participants to talk with their parents and older relatives about their family history. How long have their families been in this area? How long have they been in this country? Where did they originally come from? What brought them here? How would their experiences of settling in the area differ from those of newcomers today? How would it be similar?

Suggestion

Use the Church's early January celebration of National Migration Week to explore these issues. Compare the stories of settlers yesterday and today. Use the information, educational materials, and prayer resources provided by the USCCB's Office of Migrant and Refugee Services *(www.usccb.org/mrs)*.

Heritage

Ask participants to name the things their families do to keep their cultural heritage alive. Are there special foods? cultural music or dance traditions? other languages spoken at home? cultural approaches to celebrating holidays and holy days? photos, furniture, or other items that recall their family's heritage and history?

Suggestion

Add the participants' family and cultural traditions to your celebration of Advent, Christmas, Lent, and Easter. Incorporate these traditions into your already-scheduled seasonal events.

Values and Beliefs

Encourage participants to explore the family values and religious beliefs inherent in their family culture. What one or two values mark them as a family? How important is attention to and time with immediate family? extended family? friends? others? How are these values expressed in their religious practices? Are there any religious events or traditions unique to their culture? Are any of these given more importance by their culture than by the larger society?

Suggestion

Select an ethnic event that is celebrated by the families in your community, for example, the quinceaños (fifteenth birthday) celebration for young women of Mexican and Central American descent or the celebration of Kwanzaa. Learn about the event; experience it (or talk to someone who has), and discuss the family and religious values imbedded in the celebration.

Explore the Local Community

History

Invite the young people to gather information about the community in which they live. When was the community founded? Who were its original settlers? What were their national or ethnic backgrounds? Why did they settle there? Have other cultural groups settled in your area over time? What are the cultural, ethnic, and racial backgrounds of the newcomers to the area? How are they received in the community? What gifts, talents, traditions, and values do they bring?

Heritage

What do the various ethnic, cultural, and linguistic groups in the community do to keep their heritage and traditions alive? Where are the cultural centers in the area—the markets and stores, schools and social clubs, language and arts centers, and museums dedicated to preserving people's cultural heritage? Are special cultural events celebrated in the area (West Indian music festival, Portuguese festival honoring Saint Pio, Advent celebration of Las Posadas, for example)?

Values and Beliefs

What is the history of the people and cultures in the community? What are the national holy days and holidays? Who are their heroes and patron saints? inventors and artists?

Suggestion

The Church is, by definition, catholic, meaning universal. It incorporates all cultures and views all as gifted. Many dioceses have parishes or ministries earmarked for people of particular language groups and cultures. If there is an ethnic parish or ministry in your area, get together and do something: build community, recreate, learn and pray together, organize a joint service project, get to know one another's community and heritage. Discover the tangible and intangible things you may hold in common (values, beliefs, or traditions).

Draw on the Cultural Calendar

Starting with the cultures that are part of the parish and wider community, note days of cultural importance and interest in the ministry program calendar and parish bulletin. Use cultural events as opportunities for learning, community building, discussion, and prayer. Connect appropriate dates with related justice issues and concerns. For example, Martin Luther King Jr. Day offers a great opportunity to focus on the contributions of African Americans to American society or on the civil rights movement. The following autumn calendar is just a sampler of the cultural opportunities offered on an annual basis:

Holidays and Celebrations

- Independence Day, El Salvador and Honduras (September 15)
- American Indian Day (Fourth Friday of September)
- National Hispanic Heritage Week (third week of September)
- United Nations Day (October 24)
- Black Poetry Week (third week of October)
- Dia de los Muertos (All Souls/Day of the Dead, November 2)
- Children's Day, India (November 14)
- Diwali (Indian New Year, Hindu festival of triumph of light over darkness, November)
- opening night of Las Posadas (December 16)
- Kwanzaa (begins December 26)

Heroes and Saints

- Daniel Rudd (founded Black Catholic National Congress, born August 7)
- National Heroes Day, Philippines (August 31)
- Prudence Crandall (opened the first school for African American girls, born September 3)
- Korean Martyrs (September 20)

- Gandhi (born October 2)
- Jean-Jacques Dessaline's Day, Haiti (a founder of the Haitian republic, October 17)
- Shirley Chisholm (first African American woman elected to the U.S. House of Representatives, born November 5)
- Rosa Parks (arrested in Montgomery, AL, December 1)
- Black Elk (Native American leader, baptized a Catholic, born December 6)
- celebration of Our Lady of Guadalupe (December 12)

The Catholic Youth Bible is a great resource for prayers, cultural practices, and traditions you can use with young people. To find cultural references, go to the Article Subject Index to locate the particular culture you are researching.

You can also use the Internet to find more detailed information on various holidays, holy days, and cultural practices. Many Web sites offer a variety of resources, including recipes, prayer services, and historical background. Simply conduct a search using a keyword or phrase (for example, "Indian Independence Day").

Calendar Connections Through the Year

Overview

Sometimes there is little real choice about how and when you respond to a need for service. Empty shelves at the local food pantry and a lack of blankets at the homeless shelter call for an immediate response, as do natural disasters and the looming threat of international conflict. You pull together a project quickly to keep people from suffering any longer than is absolutely necessary.

The same can be said, at times, about justice issues. In most cases, the need is so obvious and people's interest so engaged that a programmatic response seems natural. Deciding when and how to handle other topics and project areas may not be quite as simple. Connecting with what is already happening in community life strengthens programs and provides a "hook" for recalling and reconnecting with the issue or need on a regular, annual basis. Add the events and celebrations unique to your community to the following calendar, and then use it as a tool for engaging young people in justice and service.

This is just a start on the calendar connections you can make to weave service and a concern for justice into your youth ministry throughout the year! You can use the Internet to find more detailed information on various holidays, holy days, and events. Many sites offer a variety of resources from recipes, to prayer services, to historical background. Simply conduct a search using a key word or phrase (for example, "National Arbor Day").

September Through December:
Autumn; Start of the Academic Year;
Ordinary Time, Advent, and Christmas

- Labor Day (first Monday in September)—rights of workers, living wage
- International Literacy Day (September 8)—literacy, basic right to education
- autumn equinox/fall begins (around September 23)—harvest, sharing the earth's bounty
- Feast of Saint Vincent de Paul (September 27)—concern for the poor and homeless
- Rosh Hashanah and Yom Kippur (late September through early October)—justice in the Scriptures, Reconciliation
- birthday of Mohandas Gandhi (October 2)—nonviolence, Catholic social teaching
- Feast of Saint Francis of Assisi (October 4)—environment, stewardship of Earth
- World Food Day (October 16)—human rights, hunger relief
- Feast of Saint Luke the Evangelist (October 18)—option for the poor, justice and the Scriptures
- United Nations Day (October 24)—common good, development
- All Saints and All Souls Days (November 1 and 2)—saints who lived justice and service
- Feast of Saint Martin de Porres (November 3)—patron of social action, race relations
- birthday of Dorothy Day (November 8)—Catholic Worker movement
- Veterans Day (November 11)—Catholic approaches to war and peace
- women martyrs in El Salvador (December 2)—solidarity, advocacy for the poor
- Human Rights Day (December 10)—human rights and responsibilities
- Feast of Our Lady of Guadalupe (December 12)—solidarity with the poor
- Advent—Old Testament call to justice
- Christmas—peace

List the events in your parish or community life.

January Through March:
Winter; School Break; Lent and Easter

- Emancipation Proclamation (January 1, 1863)—human rights, freedom
- World Day of Prayer for Peace (January 1)—peace
- Martin Luther King Day (third monday of January)—human rights, racism, discrimination
- Feast of Saint John Bosco (January 31)—concern for children and the poor
- birthday of Susan B. Anthony (February 15)—women's rights, faithful citizenship
- Presidents' Day (February)—faith and politics, founding principles
- Black History Month (February)—giftedness of culture, race relations
- Ash Wednesday, Lent—simple lifestyle, justice spirituality, service to those in need
- International Women's Day (March 8)—women's rights, development
- vernal equinox, spring begins (around March 21)—new life, stewardship of the earth
- National Women's History Week (second week of February)—women's history, discrimination, sexism
- Easter (March or April)—the mission of Jesus, discipleship

List the events in your parish or community life.

April Through June: Spring; End of the Academic Year; Graduations and Other Celebrations; Pentecost

- birthday of John Muir (April 21)—conservation
- Earth Day (April 22)—stewardship of creation
- National Arbor Day (last Friday in April)—ecology, environment
- Feast of Saint Joseph the Worker (May 1)—workers' rights
- Holocaust Remembrance Week (first week of May)—freedom of religion, racism
- Pentecost (May)—Church history and social justice, gifts of cultural diversity
- summer solstice, summer begins (around June 22)—alternative service vacations, respect for creation
- school graduations (May and June)—gifts given for the common good, faith and careers, service and lifestyle

List the events in your parish or community life.

June Through August: Summer; Summer Term or Break; Work and Vacation; Ordinary Time

- vacations—family service opportunities
- service-learning weeks, work camps—extended service
- Independence Day (July 4)—faithful citizenship
- bombing of Hiroshima and Nagasaki (August 7 and 9)—war and peace, just war criteria
- Feast of Saint Clare (August 11)—simple lifestyle
- Feast of Saint Maximillian Kolbe (August 14)—conscientious objection to war

List the events in your parish or community life.

Recognizing and Celebrating Youth Service

Overview

Recognizing and celebrating the accomplishments of young people are important parts of the overall service-learning experience. Recognition and celebration help make the connection between service and faith explicit and give young people, their families, and the community at large the opportunity to look at how they will move together into the future, making service and acts of justice more central in their lives. Recognizing young people's service accomplishments, then, benefits not just the young people involved, but also the larger faith community.

Benefits to Young People

Young people are looking for a community where they are accepted for who they are and recognized for the gifts they have to share. Regular signs of acceptance, affection, and affirmation help make the Church community a place they want to call home. Recognition and celebration help adolescents understand they are a vital part of the larger Church community and tell them that they are not alone in their faith journey. Involvement in service, justice, and advocacy can be time-consuming and risky—but when viewed as part of a common Christian lifestyle, this effort becomes a cause for celebration rather than concern.

Benefits to the Church Community

The faith community can benefit tremendously from the energy, enthusiasm, and sense of hope that reside in young hearts. Recognition and celebration help move young people's reflections from the personal to the communal sphere, and invite their families, friends, and fellow parishioners to take a serious look at how well they are incorporating justice and service into their lives. In fact, young people's enthusiasm for service often proves contagious, encouraging a renewed commitment from everyone involved.

Approaches to Recognizing and Celebrating Youth Service

Recognizing and celebrating young people's efforts in service and justice can take a variety of forms, formal and informal, gathered and nongathered. Select a combination of the following approaches to help celebrate the young people's growth and accomplishments:

- Keep parishioners informed of young people's service efforts through bulletin notices and parish announcements before, during, and after their involvement. If possible, list young people's names and post their pictures on the bulletin board at the back of the church or on the parish or youth program Web site.

- Encourage parishioners to ask young people about their service experience or to send notes of support and affirmation. If the service involvement is several days in length and/or involves extended planning and preparation, keep families and parishioners informed of the progress.

- During extended programs, arrange to add journal notes to the Web site daily; if feasible, add film clips and pictures to the Web site. When participants return, continue to use the Web site as a photo gallery and forum for participant and family sharing. Add prayer reflections and resources.

- Incorporate young people's service efforts into the prayers of the faithful during weekday and weekend liturgies. Invite parishioners to pray for the youth, as individuals and as a group.

- Provide families with a schedule of the service event. Offer discussion starters to help families talk through the justice issues and the experiences young people are likely to run into at the work site. Give them hints for follow-up sharing on the service involvement.

- Distribute prayer resources that will help young people and their families pray the experience together, before, during, and afterward. The longer and more demanding the service involvement, the more you should involve parents in all phases of the project.

- Inviting families, friends, and supporters to gather for a potluck supper following young people's service involvement helps focus young people's reflection on the event, gives families a chance to hear the reflections while they are still fresh, and provides a setting for prayerful recognition and celebration of young people's service efforts.

- Convert the fruits of young people's reflections (print and oral) into bulletin quotes, witness/meditative reflections during liturgy, newsletter or newspaper articles, and presentations for families, friends, religious education classes, and so forth.

- Collect participant comments and journal reflections, Scripture quotes and prayers, humorous incidents and jokes, poetry and photos into a memory and meditation book for participants.

- Catch on film the energy and effort young people put into service and post the best shots on all the available physical or electronic bulletin boards.
- Recognize particular service and justice efforts with special attention. Send participants to a week-long service event with a special blessing at weekend liturgies or a combination dinner and prayer service for families, friends, and supporters. Welcome them home with the same attention and sense of celebration. The prayer segment does not need to be long to be effective, but be sure to include the following elements:
  - Mention participants by name, and incorporate them in leadership roles during the liturgy or prayer service.
  - Select music that focuses on service and discipleship.
  - Incorporate Scripture passages that are appropriate to the project and meaningful for youth. For example, select passages that were used during the project preparation phase or are related to the type of service that the youth accomplished.
  - In opening remarks and/or the Scripture reflection, recognize service as an expression of discipleship, congratulate young people on their commitment to service, and proclaim the parish's support for their efforts.
  - Allow time for representative reflections from young people—a statement of their hopes for the project prior to the event or reflections on their experiences and learning following the program.
  - Invite family and friends to join in a special blessing for the service trip participants.

Use recognition and celebration of youth service as a forum for letting the whole parish know how truly blessed it is to have these particular young people.

Acknowledgments

The scriptural quotations contained herein are from the New Revised Standard Version Bible, Catholic Edition. Copyright © 1993 and 1989 by the Division of Christian Education of the National Council of the Churches of Christ in the United States of America. All rights reserved.

The material labeled *CFH* or *The Catholic Faith Handbook* is from The *Catholic Faith Handbook for Youth,* Brian Singer-Towns, general editor (Winona, MN: Saint Mary's Press, 2003). Copyright © 2003 by Saint Mary's Press. All rights reserved.

The material labeled *CYB* or *The Catholic Youth Bible* is from *The Catholic Youth Bible,* New Revised Standard Version, Catholic Edition (Winona, MN: Saint Mary's Press, 2000). Copyright © 2000 by Saint Mary's Press. All rights reserved.

The material labeled *CCC* is from the English translation of the *Catechism of the Catholic Church* for use in the United States of America. Copyright © 1994 by the United States Conference of Catholic Bishops (USCCB)—Libreria Editrice Vaticana. Used with permission.

The information about the goals and vision for ministry with adolescents on pages 9–10, the quotation on the purpose of ministry with adolescents on page 22, the material on the dual focus of advocacy on pages 26–27, the key points on resource 1, and the quotation on youth ministry on page 141 are from *Renewing the Vision: A Framework for Catholic Youth Ministry,* by the USCCB, Department of Education (Washington, DC: USCCB, Inc., 1997), pages 1–2, 9, 27, 27–28, 39–40, and 23, respectively. Copyright © 1997 by the USCCB, Inc. All rights reserved. Used with permission.

The extracts on page 21 and the quotation on social teaching on page 39 are from *A Century of Social Teaching: A Common Heritage, A Continuing Challenge,* by the USCCB (Washington, DC: USCCB, Inc., 1990), pages 1, 2–3, and 1, respectively. Copyright © 1990 by the USCCB, Inc. All rights reserved. Used with permission.

The "Prayer for Peace and Justice" on pages 27–28 is from *Communities of Salt and Light: Parish Resource Manual,* by the USCCB (Washington, DC: USCCB, Inc., 1994), page 52. Copyright © 1994 by the USCCB, Inc. All rights reserved. Used with permission.

Resource 2 is from *All I Really Need to Know I Learned in Kindergarten: Uncommon Thoughts on Common Things,* by Robert L. Fulghum (New York: Villard Books, 1988), pages 6–8. Copyright © 1986, 1988 by Robert L. Fulghum. Used with permission of Villard Books, a division of Random House, Inc.

Handout 1 is excerpted from *Sharing Catholic Social Teaching: Challenges and Directions, Reflections of the U.S. Catholic Bishops,* by the USCCB (Washington, DC: USCCB, Inc., 1999), pages 4–6. Copyright © 1999 by the USCCB, Inc. All rights reserved. Used with permission.

The quotation by Mother Teresa on resource 3 is from *Heart of Joy,* by Mother Teresa (Ann Arbor, MI: Servant Publications, 1987), page 6. Copyright © 1987 by José Luis Gonzalez-Balado. Published by Servant Publications. Box 9617, Ann Arbor, MI 48107. Used with permission.

The quotation by the Maryknoll Fathers and Brothers on resource 3 is from the "Mission Vision Statement," in *Maryknoll Magazine,* February 2003, at *www.maryknoll.org/MEDIA/xMAGAZINE/xmag2003/xmag02/m2s2.htm.* Used with permission.

The quotation by Dorothy Day on resource 3 is from *The Catholic Worker,* April 1964.

The quotation from Mother Teresa's Nobel Peace Prize acceptance speech in 1979 on page 50 is from *www.tisv.be/mt/en/nobel.htm,* accessed March 24, 2003.

The quotation about reordering priorities on page 58 is from *Putting Children and Families First: A Challenge for Our Church, Nation and the World,* by the USCCB (Washington, DC: USCCB, Inc., 1992), page 1. Copyright © 1992 by the USCCB, Inc. Used with permission.

The statistic about the working poor on page 63 is from *www.census.gov/ hhes/poverty/poverty01/table3.pdf,* accessed July 23, 2003.

The statistics about annual median income on pages 66–67 are from *www.usccb.org/cchd/povertyusa/tour2.htm,* accessed July 23, 2003.

The material from *Rerum Novarum,* numbers 46 and 44, by Pope Leo XIII, on page 67 is taken from *www.vatican.va/holy_father/leo_xiii/encyclicals/ documents/hf_l-xiii_enc_15051891_rerum-novarum_en.html,* accessed July 23, 2003.

The "Stone Soup" story on pages 74–75 draws on several versions of the "Stone Soup" tale, most notably that authored by Marcia Brown and first published in 1947. To read the story in full, check out *Marcia Brown, Stone Soup: An Old Tale Retold* (New York: Aladdin Books, 1986).

The prayer on handout 5 is from "The Story of Faith," in *FaithWays,* by the Center for Ministry Development (Naugatuck, CT: Center for Ministry Development, 1996), page 91. Copyright © 1996 by the Center for Ministry Development. Used with permission.

The home inspection activity in the sidebar on pages 86–87 is adapted from *Families and Youth: A Resource Manual,* edited by Leif Kehrwald and John Roberto (New Rochelle, NY: Don Bosco Multimedia, 1992), page 237. Copyright © 1992 by Salesian Society, Inc. and Don Bosco Multimedia.

The quotations on resource 6 are from *Renewing the Earth,* by the USCCB, from *Pastoral Letters and Statements of the United States Catholic Bishops, Volume VI 1989–1997,* by the USCCB (Washington, DC: USCCB, Inc., 1998), pages 397, 417, 402, 398, 398, 408, 399, 409, 409–410, 414, 410–411, and 417–418, respectively. Copyright © 1998 by the USCCB, Inc. Used with permission.

The excerpt on resource 8 is from Pope John Paul II's World Day of Peace Message, December 2001, numbers 14–15, at *www.usccb.org/pope/peacemessage.htm,* accessed July 17, 2003.

The statistics on pages 108–109 are from "Hunger in America 2001," by America's Second Harvest, a report available at *www. secondharvest.org/ whoshungry/hunger_study_intro.html,* accessed July 18, 2003.

The quotation from the United States Conference of Catholic Bishops on page 126 is from *Economic Justice for All: Pastoral Letter on Catholic Social Teaching and the U.S. Economy (1986),* by the USCCB, at *www.osjspm.org/cst/eja.htm,* accessed July 18, 2003. Copyright © 1986 by the USCCB, Inc. Used with permission.

The statistics about U.S. consumption on resource 9 are from *www.adbusters. org,* accessed July 3, 2003.

The statistics about resources and vehicles on resource 9 are from *www.global issues.org/TradeRelated/Consumption.asp,* accessed July 3, 2003.

The statistics comparing world consumption and resources to the United States' consumption and resources on resource 9 are from Catholic Relief Services, at *www.catholicrelief.org/kids,* accessed July 3, 2003.

The statistic about poverty in America on resource 9 is from the USCCB's Catholic Campaign for Human Development, at *www.usccb.org/cchd/povertyusa/ index.htm,* accessed July 3, 2003.

The remaining statistics on resource 9 are from *www.globalissues.org,* accessed July 3, 2003.